D0443387

At ✳ Issue

How Can Domestic Violence Be Prevented?

Lisa Yount, *Book Editor*

Bonnie Szumski, *Publisher*
Helen Cothran, *Managing Editor*

GREENHAVEN PRESS
An imprint of Thomson Gale, a part of The Thomson Corporation

THOMSON

GALE

Detroit • New York • San Francisco • San Diego • New Haven, Conn.
Waterville, Maine • London • Munich

LIBRARY OF CONGRESS CATALOGING-IN-PUBLICATION DATA

How can domestic violence be prevented? / Lisa Yount, book editor.
    p. cm. — (At issue)
Includes bibliographical references and index.
ISBN 0-7377-2378-5 (lib. : alk. paper) — ISBN 0-7377-2379-3 (pbk. : alk. paper)
    1. Family violence—United States—Prevention. I. Yount, Lisa. II. Series: At issue
(San Diego, Calif.)
HV6626.2.H69 2006
362.82'927—dc22   2005052766

Printed in the United States of America

Contents

Introduction

Beginning in the 1980s feminists turned a spotlight on what they said was a hidden epidemic of domestic or family violence. Most of the violence consisted of men batttering women and children, women's groups claimed, and they complained that law enforcement personnel and communities at large often saw such violence as unimportant or even acceptable. Activists' efforts to expose and condemn domestic violence, which they saw as a reflection of the inequities of a patriarchal society, resulted in such gains as the passage in 1994 of the Violence Against Women Act (VAWA), which established domestic violence, sexual assault, and stalking as federal crimes. State and local laws were also changed to make punishment of domestic violence more severe and, in some cases, mandatory. At the same time, the groups established shelters and other services that helped battered women and children find refuge from their abusers and start new lives.

Today, however, many activists and experts in the field of domestic violence have come to believe that this emphasis on rescuing women and punishing men is simplistic and may even do more harm than good. According to Linda G. Mills, a professor of social work and law at New York University, the threat of public exposure and jail time is effective mainly against batterers who have jobs and standing in their communities that they fear to lose—but these men are a minority among abusers. "Violence decreased when the persons arrested were employed, married, and Caucasian," she claims. However, when the men arrested did not fit this profile—as was most often the case—mandatory arrests often actually *increased* the likelihood of violence.

Mandatory arrest programs also often ignore the wishes of women themselves, who may not want to see their partners sent to prison. Some minority and poor women may fear the system so much that they would rather endure battering in silence than report abuse to the police. "Battered women from marginalized communities tend not to trust the legal system's ability to dispense equitable justice," writes Patricia Eng of the

Ms. Foundation for Women. Their fears are increased by the fact that in some states they as well as their batterers may be arrested and even jailed if they fight back against abuse.

Some experts are also arguing that rescuing women by providing shelters is not an effective way to prevent domestic violence. As important as shelters are, they usually can help women only after battering has taken place. At best, they may aid women in escaping further abuse. Mills and other critics say that, like punishment of abusers, rescue of the abused does little to change or even illuminate the social attitudes that contribute to domestic abuse.

Groups such as the Family Violence Prevention Fund say that the scope of efforts to stop family violence needs to broaden and that emphasis should be shifted from countering existing violence to "stopping violence before it starts." They believe that children and teens, especially those who have already experienced violence at home, need to be taught nonviolent ways of resolving conflicts and to be schooled in attitudes that recognize all people as equally worthy of respect. Girls and women need to develop self-respect and learn ways to assert their rights and control their lives. Katie Ciorba VonDeLinde and Amy Correia of the Pennsylvania Coalition Against Domestic Violence, for example, recommend providing economic education to poor women so that they can become financially independent. Women who can support themselves and their children are less likely to stay trapped in abusive relationships, they argue. Other activists say that men need to teach other men that manhood is not defined by the ability to control women and that abuse of women and children is unacceptable. "It's time for those of us who are 'well meaning men' to . . . stop colluding with other men, get out of our defined roles in society and take a stance" against domestic violence, asserts Anthony Porter, director of addiction services at Nyack Hospital in New York.

The responsibility for the prevention of domestic violence extends beyond families and the legal personnel or social workers responding to complaints, some experts argue. Rather, whole neighborhoods and communities need to be responsible for preventing domestic violence. For example, Antonia A. Vann of Asha Family Services, Inc., a nonprofit African American organization in Milwaukee that works to intervene against and prevent family violence, praises "It's Your Business," an advertising campaign developed by the Family Violence Prevention Fund. The message of that campaign, which specifically targeted African American communities, "was that domestic abuse IS everyone's issue—not a private matter, but a community issue and it is appropriate to intervene and stop the behavior," Vann notes.

Only when a wide range of groups, including health care providers, clergy, and employers, are on the lookout for signs of violence will dangerous situations be detected and potentially defused before serious damage occurs, these commentators claim. Only when communities are involved in developing educational and other programs aimed at preventing violence will the programs have the cultural sensitivity needed to make them effective. In the view of many activists, domestic violence will not end until society provides a climate in which abuse is never allowed to develop.

1

Increased Efforts Must Be Made to Prevent Domestic Violence

Janet Carter

Janet Carter is vice president of the Family Violence Preven-tion Fund and a commentator for Women's eNews, *in which this article first appeared.*

Domestic violence has become more widely recognized as a problem in the last few decades, but much more needs to be done to prevent and reduce this kind of abuse. Present responses to the problem are too simplis-tic. Instead of being encouraged to marry or remain married to their abusers, women should be helped to become self-sufficient and to protect themselves and their children from abuse. Children should be removed from abusive homes before they suffer permanent physical and mental damage. In addition, the responses of courts and social service agencies should be better co-ordinated to address the needs of both mothers and children. Finally, more effort needs to be made to edu-cate children and teens and to involve entire commu-nities in preventing future domestic violence.

Family violence defies simple, one-size-fits-all solutions. But it is clear that current U.S. prevention approaches are not adequate, and in some ways we may be heading in the wrong direction.

In his State of the Union speech [in May 2005], . . . for instance, President [George W.] Bush promoted marriage without mentioning any related initiatives on domestic violence. But coercing women into marriage without taking steps to protect them and their children from abuse is reckless and dangerous.

Certainly, we have seen some progress in the last few decades. The issue has come out of the shadows and more communities have begun to grapple with family violence and its consequences. More police officers take the issue seriously, more judges have been educated about the dynamics of abuse, more courts have improved procedures for handling family violence, more media cover the issue responsibly and, as a result, more women are seeking support and services.

More Support, More Prevention

We need to do even more to support victims. It is imperative, for instance, to ensure that women who want to leave violent homes have access to affordable housing. A recent report from the U.S. Conference of Mayors concluded that domestic violence is a primary cause of homelessness in nine cities across the country. That needs to change.

At the same time we improve services for victims, we need to find better ways to send the message that we will not tolerate abuse. To date, we have put nearly all our energy and resources into punishing batterers and helping victims. Police and courts step in after violent incidents have occurred. Shelters and other programs aid battered women and their children after they have experienced violence. And lawmakers look for ways to enhance penalties for batterers after they commit violent crimes, rather than looking for ways to prevent violence before it occurs.

> *Current U.S. [domestic violence] prevention approaches are not adequate, and in some ways we may be heading in the wrong direction.*

To make real progress in ending abuse, much more of our collective energy and resources should focus on a different phase of the problem. We should be doing more to stop violence before it starts—by teaching the next generation of boys that violence against women is always wrong; by implementing dating violence education in schools; and by encouraging parents, teachers, coaches and other adults to speak with children and teens about abuse.

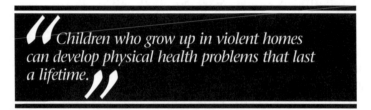

Children who grow up in violent homes can develop physical health problems that last a lifetime.

New results from one of the longest running and most respected mental health studies ever conducted confirm the need for earlier and better interventions in violent households. New data from the study, by The Simmons School of Social Work in Boston, Mass., should serve as a wake-up call to policy makers, social service systems and communities about the need to focus more on prevention strategies.

Protecting Children and Teens

Researchers running the Simmons' 25-year study of nearly 400 Massachusetts residents reported [in mid-May, 2005] . . . that family conflict and violence take a heavier toll on teens' mental health than marital disruption, divorce or separation. Male teens exposed to family conflict and violence over the years were significantly more likely than other males to have suicidal thoughts, be depressed, have emotional and behavioral problems, be drug dependent or have post-traumatic stress disorder, researchers reported. Girls from violent homes had higher rates of alcohol problems and lower grades when they graduated from high school than girls who did not experience conflict or violence in their homes.

Funded by the National Institute of Mental Health, the study confirms what domestic violence and child welfare workers have long known: Growing up in a violent home takes a terrible toll on children and teens and can cause serious, long-lasting harm.

Today millions of children in this country do grow up in violent homes. Nearly one-third of U.S. women (31 percent) report being physically or sexually abused by a husband or boyfriend at some point in their lives, according to The Commonwealth Fund, a New York-based foundation that supports independent research on health and social issues. Often, children witness or experience the abuse. In addition to mental health problems, children who grow up in violent homes can develop physical health problems that last a lifetime. And some research shows that they are more likely than other children to become victims or perpetrators of abuse.

Approaches to a Healthier Society

These grim statistics make it clear that our response to domestic violence must improve if we are to curb a problem so entrenched, costly and complex. To that end, the Family Violence Prevention Fund recommends four approaches:

Empower individuals and communities to stop violence.

Experience has taught us that neighbors, colleagues and friends can do a tremendous amount to sanction batterers and support victims. We need more involvement from men, who can talk to other men and boys and tell them that violence is unacceptable. The Family Violence Prevention Fund's groundbreaking Coaching Boys Into Men campaign run jointly with The Advertising Council was the first national campaign ever to invite men to help stop domestic violence by encouraging them to teach boys that violence against women is wrong. It was just the beginning. Individuals and communities can tell batterers their behavior is unacceptable, help battered women develop safety plans for themselves and their children, and help social service agencies identify the children and teens most in need. We can all help stop the family violence that pervades and shapes so many children's lives.

Improve the response of courts and social service agencies.

Programs and courts that address just one form of violence or abuse are less effective than those that take a multi-faceted approach. Child welfare workers are trained to address the needs of the child, while domestic violence workers look first at the needs of the battered mother. Few programs understand how to address both problems at once. The Family Violence Department at the National Council of Juvenile and Family Court Judges is working with select communities to improve the response to family violence, but change will take time. We need to accelerate the pace of change, and reform a court system that is uncoordinated, inefficient and too often fails those who urgently need its help.

Invest much more in prevention.

The Family Violence Prevention Fund is gathering sponsors for a new program in the Violence Against Women Act, which Congress will begin writing [in late 2005]. . . . It will provide funds for intervention and services for children growing up in violent homes and for the young families that are at greatest risk for violence. It will provide monies to develop, test and implement programs to help boys and young men across the nation learn to develop healthy, nonviolent relationships, with public education targeting boys. And it will train workers at Head Start, after-school and other programs to identify, aid and refer families experiencing violence to those who can help. We all need to tell Congress to make prevention a priority.

Reject programs designed to promote marriage.

The Simmons study underscores the harm that family violence causes children. It suggests that staying in a violent relationship may harm children more than divorce. Governments and communities need to help battered mothers become self-sufficient and live free of violence; not coerce them into abusive relationships through financial incentives or guilt. Lawmakers should pay attention to the Simmons study and reject the [Bush] Administration's $1.5 billion marriage promotion initiative.

This work will take time, but it is critically important. Change will mean safer families, stronger communities and a healthier society.

2

Criminalization of Domestic Violence Prevents Further Abuse

Christopher D. Maxwell, Joel H. Garner, and Jeffrey A. Fagan

Christopher D. Maxwell is an assistant professor at Michigan State University. Joel H. Garner is a researcher for the Joint Center for Justice Studies. Jeffrey A. Fagan is the director of the Center for Violence Research and Prevention at Columbia University.

Researchers have for years debated whether arresting men who perpetrate domestic violence against their wives or female intimate partners reduces subsequent abuse by these men. A recent study sponsored by the National Institute of Justice and the Centers for Disease Control and Prevention reports that arresting batterers does indeed result in a decrease in their violent aggression towards their partners. According to the study, most victims of domestic violence did not report any further abuse following the arrest (and subsequent release) of the batterers. Furthermore, most of the men had no further criminal charges for abusing their partners after their initial arrest. The findings of the study therefore support the argument that criminalizing domestic violence and arresting batterers contribute to a reduction of abuse.

A fter nearly 20 years of research designed to test the effects of arrest on intimate partner violence, questions persist on

Christopher D. Maxwell, Joel H. Garner, and Jeffrey A. Fagan, "The Effects of Arrest on Intimate Partner Violence: New Evidence from the Spouse Assault Replication Program," National Institute of Justice Research Brief, July 2001, pp. 1–2, 4–9, 13.

whether arrest is more effective at reducing subsequent intimate partner violence than such informal, therapeutic methods as on-scene counseling or temporary separation. The most important research efforts addressing this question were six experiments known collectively as the National Institute of Justice's (NIJ's) Spouse Assault Replication Program (SARP). These field experiments, carried out between 1981 and 1991 by six police departments and research teams, were designed to test empirically whether arrests deterred subsequent violence better than less formal alternatives. . . .

Previous Research

We have previously reviewed and compared the published data from the five replication sites that had reported final results to NIJ by 1993. . . . We pointed out that the comparisons were based on information drawn from different outcome measures, analytical models, and case selection criteria. Furthermore, we asserted that the inconsistency between sources and measures across sites was not necessarily because of limitations in the experimental designs, but because the SARP design called for multiple data sources and measures that could capture variations in the nature of the deterrent effect. We argued that conclusions about the deterrent effect of arrest therefore should wait until a more careful statistical analysis was completed, one based on data pooled from all five sites and using standardized measures of intervention and outcome. This Research in Brief summarizes the findings of such a statistical analysis.

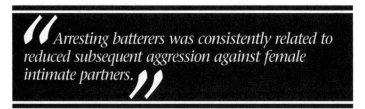

Arresting batterers was consistently related to reduced subsequent aggression against female intimate partners.

We studied the deterrent effect of arrest, using an approach that addressed many problems faced by prior efforts to synthesize the results from SARP. Supported by NIJ and the Centers for Disease Control and Prevention (CDC), the project pooled incidents from the five replication experiments, computed comparable independent and outcome measures from common data intentionally embedded in each experiment, and standardized the experimental designs and statistical models. Using the increased power of the pooled data, this study provides a more consistent, more precise, and less ambiguous estimation of the impact of arrest on intimate partner violence. Key results of this study include the following:

- Arresting batterers was consistently related to reduced subsequent aggression against female intimate partners, although not all comparisons met the standard level of statistical significance.
- Regardless of the statistical significance, the overall size of the relationship between arrest and repeat offending (i.e., the deterrent effect of arrest) was modest when compared to the size of the relationship between recidivism and such measures as the batterers' prior criminal record or age.
- The size of the reduction in subsequent intimate partner aggression did not vary significantly across the five sites. In other words, the benefit of arrest was about equal in regards to reducing aggression in all five sites.
- Regardless of the type of intervention, most suspects had no subsequent criminal offense against their original victim within the followup period, and most interviewed victims did not report any subsequent victimization by their batterer.
- This research found no association between arresting the offender and an increased risk of subsequent aggression against women. . . .

The Relationship Between Arrest and Aggression

[We conducted a] statistical analysis of the relationship between arrest and several dimensions of intimate partner aggression. The first analysis (prevalence) uses victim interview data to test for the association between arrest and any subsequent aggression during the period between the experimental incident and the last time the victim was interviewed. This model estimated that if their batterers were arrested, about 25 percent fewer female victims than expected reported one or more incidents of aggression. In other words, when the likelihood of failure (reoffending) is estimated for the typical case, about 36 percent of suspects in the arrest group reoffended, compared with 48 percent of suspects in the nonarrest group. This difference was statistically significant while controlling for differences among sites, the length of time the researchers tracked the victims, and characteristics of the suspect and incident. When examining the rates or frequency of aggression, we again found a statistically significant reduction in subsequent aggression that is related to arrest. On average, female victims whose batterers were arrested reported about 30 percent fewer incidences of subsequent aggression than expected over the followup period. Thus, we found a sizable reduction in subsequent aggression reported by victims whose batterers were assigned to the arrest group. However, because these results are based on a subsample of interviewed victims, rather than on the entire sample of eligible cases, the results from the victim interviews alone should be used with some caution because victims not interviewed may have been involved with suspects who responded differently to their intervention.

Other Factors Related to Aggression

Besides the consistent deterrent relationship between arrest and aggression, other factors were consistently related to aggression, but some factors were not. First, compared with the Omaha victims, a significantly smaller percentage of victims from the other sites (except Milwaukee) reported one or more victimizations by the suspect. On average, victims from these three sites also reported less frequent victimization. These differences in the base rates of aggression across the sites, however, did not translate into significantly different relationships between arrest and aggression in the different sites. In other words, the reduction we find in aggression reported by victims whose batterers were assigned an arrest is of about equal size in each site.

> *Female victims whose batterers were arrested reported about 30 percent fewer incidences of subsequent aggression.*

In addition to the comparisons we made across the sites, we looked for differences in aggression reported by the victims across several suspect characteristics. These comparisons found that the suspects' age and race were consistently and significantly related to the frequency of subsequent aggression as reported by the victims. These victims reported significantly less aggression when the suspect was older and nonwhite. The suspects' prior arrest records and their marital status with the victim were also consistently related to aggression, but only the prior record was significant in all but one of the analyses. Finally, several other suspect characteristics, such as employment and the use of intoxicants, were inconsistent in the direction of their relationship across the two dimensions of aggression (prevalence and frequency). For example, about 2 percent more victims of employed suspects reported one or more incidents of aggression, though these same victims simultaneously reported about 21 percent fewer incidents of aggression over the followup period.

Measuring Aggression

We next examined data collected by police departments to measure aggression by the suspect against the victim. The approach to testing whether arrest was related to officially recorded aggression follows the approach to the victim interviews, except we added a statistical analysis that examined the timing of the first new aggressive incident. Overall, the results based on the police data regarding the effectiveness of arrest are consistent in direction with those based on the victim interview data: A consistent deterrent relationship exists between arrest of the suspect and later aggression while controlling for the differences across the sites, the victim interview process, and suspect characteristics. However, the police data show a far smaller reduction in aggression because of the arrest treatment than what was detected using victim interview data, and none of these relationships reached the traditional level of statistical significance. Specifically, in the first analysis (prevalence), we found about 4 percent fewer than the expected percentage of male suspects in the arrest group with one or more incidents of subsequent aggression during the first 6 months of followup. The second analysis, which tested for the relationship between the intervention and the annual rate of aggression, found a reduction of about 8 percent from the expected number of incidents per year for suspects assigned to the arrest group. Finally, the last analysis, which examined the relationship between arrest and the timing of the first new incident, found that the expected risk of a new incident on any given day after arrest or nonarrest is reduced nearly 10 percent among the arrested suspects. Thus, depending on the dimension of the outcome, the average amount of reported aggression by the suspects dropped by between 4 and 10 percent if they were assigned to the arrest group. . . .

Arrest Deters Reoffense

The average survival [nonoffending] rate throughout the followup period varied substantially by site. On the high end was Omaha, where nearly 90 percent of the suspects had not reoffended by the end of their observation period. On the low side was Dade County, where that figure (the cumulative survival rate) was slightly less than 60 percent. These differences between sites, however, did not result in differences in survival rates by intervention group when the five sites were pooled together. . . . Throughout the followup period, which for some suspects lasted nearly 3 years, batterers who were assigned an arrest had a consistently greater rate of survival (nonoffending) than did those assigned an informal intervention.

This consistent, but small, difference in the survival rate by intervention is important because earlier analysis using data from Milwaukee suggested that arrest may have a significant long-term criminogenic effect. . . . During no particular observation period were the suspects assigned to an arrest more likely to batter their intimate partner than those in the control (nonarrest) group. Thus, among this larger sample of male intimate partner abusers, the survival rate for aggression among those assigned an arrest was never less than that of the control group. . . .

Marriage Provided No Protection

Our statistical analysis also showed that the suspects' age, race, employment status, and use of intoxicants at the time of the experimental incident were consistently and significantly related to subsequent aggression against the victim. Contrary to what we found with the victim interviews, white and employed suspects had lower levels of repeat offending according to the police records. Furthermore, suspects who were intoxicated at the time of the experimental incident and those with prior arrests for any crime had, on average, a greater likelihood of aggression recorded by the police. Only the measure of the suspect's marital status with the victim was not consistently or significantly related to aggression. Similar to what we found with the victim interview data, marriage did not appear to provide notable protection against subsequent levels of aggression. Finally, we found that the longer the researchers were able to track the victims for followup interviews, the more initial failures were reported to the police.

In addition to our findings about the relationship between arrest and aggression, we observed some patterns in the pooled data. First, we found a general pattern of cessation or termination of aggression that was only moderately related to the suspects' assigned intervention. According to officially recorded data, less than 30 percent of the suspects, arrested or not, aggressed against the same victim during the followup period. Furthermore, only about 40 percent of the interviewed victims reported subsequent victimization of any measured type by the suspects. Other studies that specifically estimated the rate of desistance from intimate violence have also found similar rates over a 1- to 2-year period.

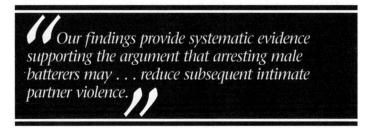

Our findings provide systematic evidence supporting the argument that arresting male batterers may . . . reduce subsequent intimate partner violence.

A second pattern concerns the high concentration of repeat aggression among a small number of batterers. During the 6-month followup, the 3,147 interviewed victims reported more than 9,000 incidents of aggression by the suspects since the initial incident. While most victims reported no new incidents of aggression, about 8 percent of them reported a total number of incidents that represented more than 82 percent of the 9,000 incidents. The same 8 percent also accounted for 28 percent of the 1,387 incidents recorded by the police that involved an interviewed victim. . . .

Arrest Decreases Violence Against Women

Our multisite pooled analysis of the five replication experiments found good evidence of a consistent and direct, though modest, deterrent effect of arrest on aggression by males against their female intimate partners. The victim interviews indicate that the arrest of the suspect and any subsequent confinement, when compared with the alternative interventions collectively, significantly reduced the expected frequency of subsequent aggression by 30 percent. Similarly, arrest may have reduced by a smaller amount the number of times the police responded to subsequent domestic violence incidents involving the same victim and suspect and may have extended the time between the initial incident and the first subsequent incident. . . .

The findings of this research have several implications for policy. First, our findings provide systematic evidence supporting the argument that arresting male batterers may, independent of other criminal justice sanctions and individual processes, reduce subsequent intimate partner violence. The size and statistical significance of the effect of arrest varied depending on whether the subsequent aggression was measured by victim interviews or police records; even so, in all measures (prevalence, frequency, rate, and time-to-failure), arrest was associated with fewer incidents of subsequent intimate partner aggression. This finding exists during the first several days after the experimental incident regardless of the period of detention, as well as beyond 1 year. The arrested suspects were detained an average of 9 days, but the reduction in aggression associated with arrest did not vary by the length of the suspects' detention. Thus, our research finds no empirical support for the argument that arrest may eventually increase the risk for violence against women. . . .

While arrest reduced the proportion of suspects who reoffended and the frequency with which they reoffended, arrest did not prevent all batterers from continuing their violence against their intimate partners. In fact, we found a small number of victims who have chronically aggressive intimate partners. Future research needs to build on preliminary efforts to accurately predict high-rate repeat offenders and to find methods of helping their victims before they are victimized further.

3

Criminalization of Domestic Violence Does Not Prevent Further Abuse

Linda G. Mills

Linda G. Mills is a professor at New York University's Ehren-kranz School of Social Work. She is also an affiliated professor of law at the New York University School of Law and vice provost for university life and interdisciplinary initiatives. Her books include The Heart of Intimate Abuse: New Interventions in Child Welfare, Criminal Justice, and Health Settings.

During the last decades of the twentieth century, mainstream feminists pushed to have domestic violence prosecuted as a criminal act. In their opinion, violence is almost always a reflection of women's oppression by a patriarchal society. The feminists' efforts increased public awareness of domestic violence and lowered tolerance for it, but their views are simplistic and ignore the role and choices of women involved in abusive relationships. The criminalization approach, furthermore, not only does not reduce domestic violence in many cases but may sometimes make violent situations worse. Instead of distancing themselves from domestic violence by automatically placing it in the hands of the legal system, people need to look at the problem more thoughtfully and attempt to understand its complexity.

Linda G. Mills, *Insult to Injury: Rethinking Our Responses to Domestic Abuse.* Princeton, NJ: Princeton University Press, 2003. Copyright © 2003 by Princeton University Press. Reproduced by permission.

Walking down Bethnal Green Road, an arterial street in working-class East London, I witnessed a remarkable scene. I was carrying my laundry and talking with a friend when my focus was drawn to a mother walking with her five-year-old son. He was demanding attention, as all children do, and her patience suddenly snapped. She whipped around and smacked him across the face. He staggered backward. I was shocked that I was witnessing this violence at such close range and simultaneously struck by its intimacy and familiarity. I had just watched a mother assault a child in broad daylight in the middle of a crowded public street. I felt sad for the child and angry with a mother who would treat her child this way. Before I could respond, the child collected himself and, to my astonishment, stepped forward and punched his mother in the stomach.

I turned and looked at my companion; we were both impressed and somewhat pleased that the child had asserted his rights, stood up for himself, and retaliated. Then it slowly dawned on me. In that split second, we had witnessed the genesis of intimate abuse. This was an unexceptional everyday scene, just another parent who felt entitled to correct her child with physical admonitions and a child who reacted unreflectively. But the little boy would grow up to become a man, and he was already being taught to respond to women with violence. We learn to become violent, as this scene suggests, but we seldom realize that is what we are learning, let alone that it is what we are teaching.

The image of that altercation has stayed with me for many years. We all witness and experience violence in our lives. We have all become habituated to violence, consciously or unconsciously judging who is right and wrong in relation to violence. . . .

Denying and Projecting

Becoming conscious of violence is always met with resistance. We have a hard time believing violence is occurring, even when it is direct and personal. We tend to run, either literally or metaphorically, so as to ignore it or put it behind us. Denial kicks in, and we are left pretending it never happened.

The only time we are truly comfortable thinking about violence is when it affects other people. Then we become experts on violence and on what other people should do about it. Our denial and paralysis in the face of our own experience gets externalized: we solve the problems of others while denying our own. When our anger is exteriorized in this way, it is projected: what we cannot accept in our own past, we project onto others.

Consider the reaction of a man who grew up with a violent mother. If he is unaware of his history or how it affects his view of violence, he might project his unconscious hatred of his own mother onto the woman on Bethnal Green Road. He might villainize her without any attempt to understand or engage her. Now assume he is also a social worker; he might believe that the child is best served by taking him away from his mother. It is highly unlikely that he would have any awareness that his judgment was determined, in some significant way, by his own unacknowledged prior experiences of violence. When we project, we judge someone else for what happened to us; we act out our rage at our own helplessness by controlling what others do. . . .

> **//** We have all become habituated to [domestic] violence, consciously or unconsciously judging who is right and wrong in relation to violence. **//**

Returning to the five-year-old boy, it is significant that my initial response was supportive of his physical reaction to his mother's violence. I identified with the child's helplessness, with his vulnerability in the face of abuse by an adult. Most of us feel that identification when we see a child struck or otherwise abused. The reality of the situation is much more complicated. Here a mother is "coaching" a child to be abusive, teaching her son to react violently toward women. I am sure we would not normally view the situation in this vein.

On reflection, what is most remarkable about this interaction is the complexity of violence between intimates; it crosses genders and generations. Unless we appreciate the dynamics of intimate abuse, we will judge it before attempting to understand it. Consider this disturbing fact: after a few years have passed and the boy who hit his mother on Bethnal Green Road has become a man, it is statistically likely that he will hit a woman again. At that time, some people, especially a group called "mainstream feminists," will argue for his arrest and prosecution. What is perhaps most troubling about this situation is that mainstream feminists would at the same time leave the mother blameless. Paradoxically, mainstream feminists are arguing in this situation for the disempowerment of the violent mother and the empowerment of the violent man. The mother, viewed as a victim, is without blame. The man is the cause and the sum of the violence he inflicts. The mother's contribution to his trained reaction to women is ignored. In the most traditional of terms, he is everything, and she is nothing.

An Oversimplified View

Historically, mainstream feminism's highly successful response to heterosexual domestic violence has been to ignore the complexity of the dynamic that I witnessed. The child whom I saw being hit by his mother is three times more likely to become violent in intimate relationships than a child who was not hit. The moment that he hits a woman, mainstream feminists have legislated that he be taken out of the context of his biography and into an automatic legal process in which he will be held absolutely accountable for any violence he committed. He will be defined as a product of patriarchy, and his masculine privilege will account for the sole source of his aggression. For many mainstream feminists, the causal relationship between patriarchy and violence is uniform and singular; heterosexual men beat women because of patriarchy. Domestic violence involves perpetrator and victim, and nothing more. While this makes for easy policy and uniform legislative solutions, it addresses the symptoms of intimate abuse and not its causes. . . .

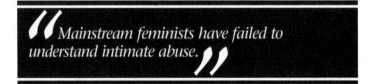

Mainstream feminists have failed to understand intimate abuse.

It is my belief, arrived at over two decades of working in the field of intimate violence, that mainstream feminists have failed to understand intimate abuse and the choices women make when they are involved in abusive relationships. To my sorrow, I have come to realize that, in general, the mainstream feminist response to domestic violence represents the views of a relatively small minority of women who have the resources and political strength to aggressively assert their narrow explanations for domestic violence. Whether by virtue of denial, projection, or privilege, mainstream feminists have been able to advocate for a uniform, and ironically conservative, law-and-order response to intimate abuse that blames men and ultimately treats women as innocent victims. Consider a [2002] New York City ad campaign that features pictures of men behind bars. On billboards, subway trains, and government Web sites, we see the following captions: "Successful Executive. Devoted Churchgoer. Abusive Husband." "Big Man on Campus. Star Athlete. Abusive Boyfriend." "Employee of the Month. Soccer Coach. Wife Beater." At first blush these ads seem at the very least paradoxical. If these men are successful leaders in their fields, why are they behind bars? On reflection it seems shocking that the only response available is imprisonment and shame. Can it really be asserted that their abusive behaviors are all that matter? Is it really not possible, even with successful men, to work their violence through? The mainstream law-and-order response here seems to wholly fail to address the problem; it simply wants to lock it away.

A Failing Approach

What may come as a surprise to many people is that study after study confirms that arrest, prosecution, and incarceration do not necessarily reduce the problem of domestic violence and may even be making the problem worse. Arrest has been shown to have a positive deterrent effect on men who are "good-risk" perpetrators, that is, people who have something to lose by being incarcerated. On the other hand, the men most likely to be arrested because of the criminal justice system's inherent class and race bias can become more violent in response to arrest. Even a coordinated response that includes arrest, prosecution, and incarceration has not shown better outcomes. Although there are conflicting results, no study documents an overwhelming reduction in intimate violence in the groups most likely to be arrested. At worst, the criminal justice system increases violence against women. At best, it has little or no effect.

The assumptions underpinning mainstream feminist advocacy efforts are that all intimate abuse is heterosexual, that violence is a one-way street (male to female), that all violence warrants a state response, and that women want to leave rather than stay in their abusive relationships. It is on this basis that mainstream feminists advocated for interventions that called for the state to arrest and prosecute batterers regardless of the woman's wishes. Mandatory arrest and prosecution, as they have come to be called, became the battle cry of mainstream feminists. Their efforts were overwhelmingly successful.

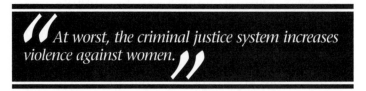

At worst, the criminal justice system increases violence against women.

Their success was important and drastically lowered the level of social tolerance for domestic violence and focused attention on the pervasiveness and danger of intimate abuse. Their success, no doubt, immobilized some men who were so violent that they would otherwise have killed their intimate partners. It is important however, to distinguish between that end of the spectrum that sociologist Michael Johnson dubs "patriarchal terrorism," and "common couple violence," which reflects the more common dynamic. . . . My argument is that recognizing that some men inflict severe physical and emotional violence on women is important, but in many cases it is neither the whole story of violence in that relationship, nor the most common instance of violence in the intimate sphere. . . .

A Need for Reflection

Only by looking at the violence—its complexity, its history, its tendrils throughout our culture—can we begin to understand, address, and ameliorate our relationship to it.

I believe that although on the surface a lot has changed in relation to intimate abuse over the last thirty years, the work has largely focused on casting the abuse as violence against women. Although in some instances this accurately characterizes the phenomenon, it is far from the whole story. Recognizing that we all have narratives of intimate abuse and corresponding experiences with violence partly explains why we have responded so vehemently to the problem. This recognition provides a starting point for a more informed and less judgmental practice. It also provides an opportunity to rethink the limitations of our current strategies and to reformulate our current theories of intimate abuse. . . .

The history of feminist responses to intimate abuse has precluded any adequate understanding of the complexity and intimacy of violence in domestic relationships. Yet developing an adequate feminist theory is the most practical of current tasks. To understand violence we need to situate ourselves in relation to it and acknowledge, reflect on, and work through those aspects of our experiences that get replicated in our judgment of violence in others. It is striking and shocking that the violence that I witnessed on Bethnal Green Road was the violence of a mother against a child, female against male, and one generation against the next. We face a choice: either, as historically has happened, we can prejudge this violence and so turn away and run from it. Or . . . we can walk toward the violence and endeavor to understand and work through it.

Everything is at stake. The boy will become a man, and another generation's relationship to violence will be defined. His mother will be exonerated, and his wife will be labeled a victim. His children might be the recipients of his or even her violence, and/or might become violent themselves. No one will seize the opportunity offered, each time intimate abuse occurs, to stop and reflect on the violence and, as I am suggesting, seize the chance to do something about it.

4

Restraining Orders Prevent Domestic Violence

Steve Twomey

Steve Twomey is a columnist for the Washington Post.

Although restraining orders cannot protect every victim of domestic violence, they have made life safer for thousands of women. Studies have shown that women who obtain protection orders are less likely to be contacted, threatened, or hurt by their abusers than women who do not do so. Penalties for violating restraining orders are more severe than they used to be, and police are more likely to arrest men for violations. The potential shame of public exposure as well as legal penalties help to keep all but the worst abusers from going against such orders. The process of going to court to obtain a restraining order can also aid battered women by exposing them to resources and services, such as assistance in finding housing or jobs, that can help them respond to or escape from abusive situations.

Wanda Pasha, among thousands of others, got one.
In some locales nationwide, it's dubbed a restraining order, in others a civil protection order. Whatever the place or the jargon, such orders are designed to keep an abusive man—it's almost always a male—away from a frightened woman, as if language alone can serve as a moat around a life.

Pasha got her paper on April 27, [2003].

Yet four months later, violence came to her Piscataway [New Jersey] home anyway. Pasha, a child of Amiri Baraka, a former poet laureate of New Jersey, was elsewhere, in Las Vegas, on vacation. Instead, it was her sister and her sister's friend, having stopped by to pick up a few things, who were found [in mid-August, 2003] in the Martin Lane split-level, both shot again and again. The only suspect named by police, though not charged: James Coleman, Wanda Pasha's estranged husband and the object of the April 27 stay-clear order.

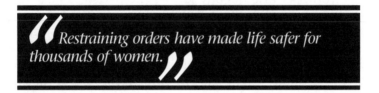

Restraining orders have made life safer for thousands of women.

It would be easy to advertise the double-homicide as slam-dunk proof that words are no bulwark against spurned, controlling and volatile partners, and that only the naive would bother to traipse to court believing they are enough.

An easy assessment, but simplistic.

A Path to Protection

In the last two decades, a legal system that used to write off domestic spats as let-them-work-it-out affairs has gotten far more aggressive, and fresh research suggests that restraining orders have made life safer for thousands of women, even if not all women, even if not two women in a Piscataway house.

"We certainly wouldn't get rid of (protection orders) in a million years," said Sandy Clark, assistant director of the New Jersey Coalition for Battered Women. "Many, many men will listen to what a restraining order has to say."

Oddly, the orders might be saving abusers, too.

Instances of women killing their batterers as a desperate form of final relief are dropping, said Susan L. Keilitz, a Virginia-based consultant and researcher, and restraining orders are probably a reason. They give women a sense of control over their circumstances, and allies in the guise of the courts and police.

Indeed, nearly three-quarters of some 285 women who obtained a protection order said their lives improved in the month after they went to court, according to a 1998 study by a team led by Keilitz. By six months later, even more—85 percent—felt the restraining order had helped.

"A woman should definitely bother to go get one," Keilitz said.

That is, if it feels right.

Taking Violence Seriously

Advocates do not flatly urge every abused woman to seek the protection of the law, preferring to let each evaluate what might work, because nobody knows the batterer's personality better than his victim. But another telling study, published [in July 2003], found that abused women who did get protection orders had "significantly" less risk of being contacted by the abuser. They were less likely to be threatened with a weapon by him, and less likely to be hurt by him, according to the study in the *American Journal of Preventive Medicine*.

Victoria L. Holt, a professor at the University of Washington who led the study, said that when she discusses its findings with officials at Seattle shelters for battered women, they often scoff, because shelters are full of girlfriends, wives and ex-wives who got protection orders to no avail. The study's authors also acknowledge that their results did not match those of a 1985 study that found restraining orders didn't do much good.

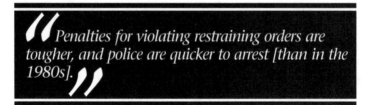

Penalties for violating restraining orders are tougher, and police are quicker to arrest [than in the 1980s].

But they have a ready answer for that discrepancy: Much has changed since 1985. Penalties for violating restraining orders are tougher, and police are quicker to arrest, often because laws now require them to do so. Clark, of the New Jersey Coalition for Battered Women, said there are "light years" of difference between today's official attitudes toward domestic violence and those of decades past.

In Piscataway, for example, the department's 90 police officers must attend domestic-violence refresher sessions twice a year, reviewing guidelines, scenarios and changes in the law. They will even help a woman obtain a restraining order, said Capt. Richard Ivone, a spokesman.

"That piece of paper only has teeth, only has any power . . . if the perpetrator really believes the criminal justice system is taking this seriously," says Juley Fulcher, public policy director of the National Coalition Against Domestic Violence, and "from what I can see, it looks like a lot more judges are providing serious consequences and a lot more oversight is occurring as well."

Not only are many men deterred by the criminal charges they would face if they persist in calling, stalking or visiting a woman in defiance of a court order, they comply because they are ashamed that their private actions have become public knowledge—and could get more so if they violate the order. Far from being a career criminal, a drug addict or a bum, the abuser often has a job, status and a family to lose. "Probably he doesn't want anyone to know he's in court . . . or he's just embarrassed," said Jacki Marich, executive director of Women Aware in Middlesex County [New Jersey].

Restraining orders can defuse in a tangential way, too. Merely by going to court to get an order, women learn about a range of services—counseling, shelters, job help, support groups—that might help them deal with an abuser and an abusive situation, Keilitz said.

Still, abuse remains a huge problem, with 82,373 incidents reported in New Jersey in 2001, the last year for which numbers are available. Some 13,000 restraining orders were issued, Clark said. Twenty-six women were murdered. If there is anything positive about the numbers, it is that the totals don't change much from year to year, even though the population of the state has risen.

Need for More Aggressive Action

Advocates for abused women also worry that, despite all the progress, too many judges and police officers aren't tough enough or trained enough. A 1998 task force found that although New Jersey's domestic violence laws and policies "are among the toughest in the nation," too many police officers were still discouraging victims from filing complaints and too many judges were insensitive toward them. Even [in 2003], five years later, "I certainly see many cases where I wished the police had been more aggressive," Clark said.

There is, too, a cohort of men so violent and so unstable that they are rarely intimidated by restraining orders. A study in the *American Journal of Public Health*, also published [in July 2003], suggests that a woman's chances of being killed increase considerably if the abuser is unemployed, has access to a gun and has already made violent threats.

James Coleman reportedly lost his job as a Newark city health investigator in June [2003]. In that month, too, he showed up at the Piscataway house, pointed a gun at Wanda Pasha's head and said, "I should kill you," according to police.

It is not clear whether, by then, Coleman had been served with the April restraining order, which came after police responded at least five times to reports of disturbances at the Piscataway house and after Wanda Pasha reportedly told Coleman, her husband of three years, to get out. But the alleged threat with a gun prompted police to issue a warrant for Coleman on charges of aggravated assault and terroristic threats.

Ivone, the Piscataway police spokesman, would not comment on the specific steps the department then took to find Coleman. Nor would Newark police, who were asked for help, comment on what they did. Given the allegations against Coleman and the history between him and Pasha, "This would be a person you'd want on your No. 1 priority list," said Clark.

The police never found him. He turned himself in after the homicides.

A Coleman family spokesman, Emmanuel Avraham, has said Coleman has proclaimed his innocence. "He said 'my wife and I may have had problems, but I would never have done this,'" Avraham said. "He said he's very saddened by the loss of his sister-in-law and the other young lady."

5

Restraining Orders Do Not Prevent Domestic Violence

Ken Little

Ken Little is a staff reporter for the Star-News *in Wilmington, North Carolina. He specializes in stories on crime and courts.*

A protective or restraining order is a court order that forbids a person from carrying out an action that is likely to threaten or harm someone. In domestic violence cases, a typical restraining order might forbid an alleged abuser from coming within a certain distance of, or even having any kind of contact with, a woman who claims that that person has harmed or threatened her. However, protective orders are civil rather than criminal legal procedures, and most of the burden of their enforcement falls on the shoulders of potential victims rather than on the legal system. Protective orders do not entitle police to search potential offenders' homes or remove weapons, for instance. In addition, law enforcement personnel can act on restraining orders only if the person who took out an order complains that it has been violated. Courts and prosecutors need to increase the number of officers available to respond to domestic violence calls and should also help victims fill out forms and prepare for court appearances. Both victims and perpetrators in domestic abuse cases involving restraining orders need to be taught better ways to handle their relationships.

Johan B. Peck had no trouble buying an assault rifle April 26, [2004], just hours after Christen Naujoks took out a domestic violence protective order against the convicted felon.

On June 4, [2004], Mr. Peck used the same weapon to shoot his 22-year-old former girlfriend 11 times in front of her apartment building in northern New Hanover County, [North Carolina]. The conditions of the protective order specifically prohibited Mr. Peck from buying or keeping a gun, yet he was able to circumvent federal law and purchase the rifle despite convictions for crimes against nature and assault on a female.

Robert Hewson did not have a criminal past, but the protective order taken out against him Sept. 9, [2004], by wife Gail Tice clearly stated Mr. Hewson was not to possess, own or receive any firearms. Mr. Hewson, who was estranged from Ms. Tice, did not turn in the handgun used Sept. 29 to kill the 67-year-old real estate agent inside her Landfall [N.C.] home.

Guns were readily available in each case, and the shooters did not hesitate to use them.

Protective orders often forbid having firearms, but the authorities probably don't know whether the defendant is complying. Law enforcement officials say it is often left up to the defendant to turn in his weapons. There's generally no search of his home or car.

A protective order is a civil action, not a criminal charge. That means its enforcement is largely on the shoulders of the person who fears for her safety—she must report a violation, and then it becomes a criminal matter.

Too Many Loopholes

Advocates for victims of domestic violence say change is needed to close loopholes in the system.

Holly Naujoks, Christen's mother, pointed out flaws [in October 2004] as she spoke about domestic violence at a "Take Back the Night" rally in Wilmington, [N.C.]. Mrs. Naujoks described the difficulties Christen had obtaining a protective order and the way Mr. Peck manipulated the system.

"First of all, I do believe in a protection order," Mrs. Naujoks said . . . in a telephone interview from her Ohio home. "That is all we have right now. We can build on it to make it stronger and protect more women."

Because her daughter also had taken out a criminal charge of harassment against Mr. Peck, the system should have ensured that he was in custody by the time he acted on his plan to kill Christen, Mrs. Naujoks said.

It seems the victim has fewer rights than the person causing the domestic violence situation, she said.

"When we went in there to get the protective order, we didn't know the process. We didn't have an advocate," she said. "We needed someone to go through it with us and explain the pros and cons."

No one anticipated the determination of Mr. Peck to take Christen Naujoks' life, said Clarke Speaks, her lawyer.

A protective order is a civil action, not a criminal charge.

"The day that we got that protective order, he left the courthouse with that protective order in his hand, and he bought the weapon somewhere," Mr. Speaks said. "The only thing I think you can do that would have protected Christen short of getting out of this place is remove him from society and lock him up somehow, and you can't lock him up because of suspicion."

But Mr. Peck, who was on probation for his previous offenses, had been charged with harassment in connection with Ms. Naujoks' case—something the civil court apparently wasn't aware of, her mother said.

"The District Attorney's Office was not aware John was back in the system again and his probation could have been revoked if he was charged with harassment," Mrs. Naujoks said. "You should have had the court system and the probation officer meeting together."

Limited Enforcement Power

There were 461 domestic violence protective orders issued . . . between Jan. 1 and July 29, [2004], in New Hanover County, according to the N.C. Administrative Office of the Courts. During that same period there were 274 orders issued in Brunswick County and 87 in Pender County.

Once a protective order is issued, the matter is basically out of a judge's hands, said John J. Carroll III, chief District Court judge for the Fifth Judicial District, which encompasses New Hanover and Pender counties.

"The sheriff's department has to serve the defendant. The only way you're going to know if it is being enforced or not is the plaintiff," Judge Carroll said. "It's a civil action."

Those serving the orders have limited enforcement options. A search warrant, which can be a tool in criminal cases, is not an option in a civil matter.

"A lot of people are under the conception that the order allows us to forcibly search the residence and seize weapons. It doesn't allow us to do that," said Detective J.C. Anderson, a New Hanover County deputy who works with the District Attorney's Office domestic violence unit.

"If a defendant has threatened the use of the weapon, the judge can order surrender of a weapon within 24 hours. If he doesn't surrender it, he can be charged with a felony," Detective Anderson said.

Compliance can be difficult to ascertain.

The defendant could tell the deputy serving the order that he gave his guns to someone else, Judge Carroll said. Unless the deputy sees a weapon or has reason to suspect a crime in progress, he can't search the premises, the judge said.

A protective order can only go so far, Judge Carroll acknowledged.

"If they have it in their mind to harm someone, it isn't going to stop them," he said.

Flawed Background Checks

Flaws in the country's background check system often make it easy for those convicted of crimes to buy a weapon.

Nearly 3,000 domestic abusers bought firearms between 1998 and 2001, a U.S. General Accounting Office study shows. According to the Office of Justice Programs in the Department of Justice, 40 percent of women killed with firearms are murdered by an intimate partner.

Because of his felony record, Mr. Peck should not have owned a gun under any circumstances, Interim District Attorney John Sherrill said.

In Mr. Peck's case, the 2001 assault on a female and crimes against nature convictions in connection with incidents involving a previous girlfriend did not prevent him from buying the assault rifle used to kill Ms. Naujoks from a private dealer.

Such weapons are readily available at gun shows and through classified ads. Background checks required at gun shops would likely have resulted in a denial for Mr. Peck, authorities said.

Even with federally and state-assisted programs like "Project Safe Neighborhoods," aimed at taking armed criminals off the streets, the system remains ill-equipped to keep guns out of the hands of those intent on domestic violence, New Hanover County Sheriff Sid Causey said.

Once a protective order is issued, the matter is basically out of a judge's hands.

"In 15 or 20 minutes, I think you can find a handgun on a street corner if you're a local or a regular person. Getting weapons is not a problem. It has never been a problem," he said.

Mr. Peck was obsessive in his desire to control Christen Naujoks' life, Mrs. Naujoks said.

"A person like John Peck was hell-bent on killing Christen. He wanted revenge on Christen, so no amount of paper was going to keep her safe. Most people aren't like that," she said.

"Most people do comply with a judge's orders. Are there cases where they don't? We've seen that," Mr. Sherrill said. "You're talking about a pretty good volume of cases where people get guns and kill people. It's a tragedy, and we're looking at everything we can do to prevent that. We take domestic violence cases seriously."

Some victims, like 17-year-old Aziya McLaughlin, never get to file a protective order. When the New Hanover High School teenager broke up with boyfriend Derrick Allen, Mr. Allen, 20, persisted in calling and following her. Sheriff's deputies said Mr. Allen used a .38 caliber revolver stolen in a March 2003 burglary at a New Hanover County home to shoot Aziya on Oct. 26, [2004], and then kill himself minutes later.

Improving the System

The National Crime Prevention Council is among agencies that track domestic crimes involving firearms.

"When a domestic abuser is arrested, he or she can often be lost in the shuffle through overextended courts. Because the threat or use of a firearm is the number one indicator of future domestic homicide, it is important that these cases are flagged and monitored as soon as they come to the attention of the criminal justice system," a Crime Prevention Council strategy paper recommends. . . .

The N.C. General Assembly passed a law in 2003 that makes it a felony to possess a firearm when a domestic violence protective order is in effect.

"There's no question a protective order can only protect folks when a person is going to follow the orders of the court," Mr. Sherrill said. "We try to make the system as victim-friendly as we can to try and monitor the defendant."

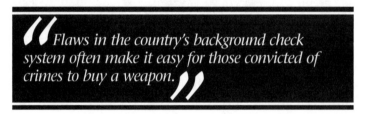

Flaws in the country's background check system often make it easy for those convicted of crimes to buy a weapon.

Domestic violence victims can receive assistance in filling out paperwork, Mr. Sherrill said. A witness coordinator will also meet with a victim before any court appearance. Mrs. Naujoks said no one met with Christen until 10 minutes before her court appearance.

Mr. Speaks said the District Attorney's Office could have a representative present when domestic violence-related cases are being heard to explain to victims how civil and criminal charges against a defendant may interact.

"Maybe they could help educate the victims. (Christen) was, and the fact is it didn't change anything," Mr. Speaks said.

"I just think if somebody is dead-set on ending anyone's life, they can do it and I don't know if there is anything that can be put in place," he said. "My reaction now would be to tell them to get in their car and drive until they run out of gas and get some more gas and then drive some more."

District Attorney-elect Ben David said changes are already being made in the approach to domestic violence taken by his office.

"We're going to reorganize the office a little bit, so when people walk into that unit they know directly who they're dealing with," he said.

Mrs. Naujoks, who has spoken out on domestic violence issues since her daughter's death, has a number of suggestions to improve the system. Among them are making sure arrest warrants are served in a timely manner and that safeguards be created to ensure that all paperwork goes to the right court and judge.

People such as Mr. Peck, who was going to a court-mandated anger management class monitored by probation, also need to attend a course addressing domestic violence, Mrs. Naujoks said.

"It should be automatic that the person who a protective order is taken out against should go to a class and learn about control," she said. "It should be mandatory that they learn how to break up with somebody."

Christen Naujoks, her mother said, had never met a troubled person like Mr. Peck before and didn't have the tools to cope with his actions.

"The person who files the protective order should have classes on how to get out of an unhealthy relationship and a relationship that is controlling," Mrs. Naujoks said.

Domestic violence cases should be overseen by one person who is aware of all the aspects of that case, she said.

In helping to protect other domestic violence victims, something positive may yet come out of the death of her daughter, Mrs. Naujoks said.

"I don't want my daughter's death to be in vain," she said. "John knew more of what was going on and had more rights and more knowledge than Christen did, and it should be the other way around."

6

Batterer Intervention Programs Can Prevent Domestic Violence

Edward W. Gondolf

Edward W. Gondolf is director of research at the Mid-Atlantic Addiction Training Institute, part of the Indiana University of Pennsylvania.

Courts often assign people arrested for or convicted of domestic violence to batterer intervention programs, counseling programs aimed at changing the batterers' attitudes and preventing further abuse. An evaluation of batterer intervention programs at different sites concluded that such programs can reduce the likelihood that abuse will be repeated, but that "the system"—the context in which a program is administered—is at least as important as the program itself in determining effectiveness. Programs are more likely to reduce abuse when, for instance, court referral of batterers to the programs is swift and certain and when the court or probation officers review batterers' progress frequently. Programs of short duration often work as well as longer ones. The chief problem with all batterer intervention programs is that about 20 percent of the men who attend them continue to abuse their spouses repeatedly in spite of the programs. Unfortunately, these repeat assaulters are difficult to identify in advance. Batterer intervention programs can prevent domestic violence and deserve to be continued. However, the community and legal system needs to hold men accountable if these programs are to be truly effective.

O ur multisite evaluation [of batterer intervention programs] has been a long and sometimes complicated journey. In our attempt to address limitations and issues of previous program evaluations, we have discovered some new areas to consider. Our examination of reassault rates and women's perceptions, for instance, presents a more positive picture than previous evaluations and an implicit endorsement of conventional batterer counseling. How could that be? Our findings about the reassault trends and the repeat reassaulters, moreover, suggest the need for more system development. More needs to be done before and after batterer programs as part of this process. The emphasis on system development contrasts with the heightened attention [of other researchers] on new counseling approaches and innovations. . . .

> *[After their batterers attended intervention programs] a de-escalation of violence and abuse appears to have benefited more of the women [in abusive relationships].*

The major implication is that *the system matters.* Batterer program outcome is, for instance, likely to be improved with swift and certain court referral, periodic court review or specialized probation surveillance, and ongoing risk management. . . .

Encouraging Outcomes

Our multisite evaluation of batterer intervention has revealed some encouraging and instructive results. Men who were arrested and enrolled in batterer programs appeared to be affected by the intervention. The vast majority of the men did eventually stop their violence for a sustained period of time. Although nearly half the men reassaulted their partners sometime during the 4-year follow-up, most of the first-time reassault occurred in the 9 months following program intake. During this period, the men were still participating in programs or expected to be in programs. At 2½ years after program intake, more than 80% of the men had not assaulted their female partners in the previous year. At 4 years after program intake, more than 90% had not been violent for at least a full year.

There also appears to have been a reduction in the severity of abuse. Approximately three quarters of the men had severely assaulted their partners in the past (i.e., an average of 3 years prior to the program intake). Less than a quarter of the men had severely assaulted their partners in the 4 years after program intake. These severe assaults tended to result in physical injuries of mostly bruises; only 5% of the women sought medical treatment for their injuries. Other forms of abuse, such as controlling behavior, verbal abuse, and threats, also showed a sharp decline over time, although they did not decrease to the extent of reassault. Most encouraging was that the vast majority of the women felt "very safe," believed it was very unlikely that their partners would hit them again, and rated their quality of life to be improved overall. In sum, a *de-escalation* of violence and abuse appears to have benefited more of the women.

A downside to the intervention has emerged, however. Although the majority of men eventually stopped their violence, a portion of men (approximately 20%) repeatedly reassaulted their partners during the follow-up. These men were responsible for most of the injury. Despite our varied attempts to identify and distinguish these men, the *repeat reassaulters* were difficult to differentiate from the men who did not reassault or reassaulted only once during the follow-up. Prediction of the outcomes using information assessed at program intake was, in general, negligible. The main *risk markers* were the ones criminologists have regularly found with violent offenders: severe previous assault, the extent of one's criminal record, and a severe mental disorder. The best risk markers overall were the women's predictions of reassault and the man's drunkenness during the follow-up.

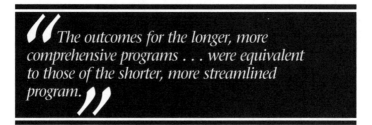

The outcomes for the longer, more comprehensive programs . . . were equivalent to those of the shorter, more streamlined program.

In brief, our research team did not find any evidence that risk assessment instruments or other risk factors would in themselves be able to identify reassault at a success rate acceptable to practitioners. The most important finding may be that the repeat reassaulters got away with their behavior. That is, they were not apprehended or not sufficiently contained after their first reassault. Increased feedback from the women and ongoing monitoring, especially of alcohol use and repeat abuse, would probably be the most effective way to manage the risk of reassault.

The components of the intervention system as a whole are: arrest, court action, probation supervision, victims' services, and other community services, along with the batterer-counseling programs. The answer to the question. "Do batterer programs add an effect beyond the other intervention components?" appears to be "yes." There was a substantial difference between those men who attended a program for less than 2 months (dropouts) and those men who attended for 2 months or more. This reassault difference remained significant when we controlled for possible demographic, relationship, personality, and behavioral differences between the program *dropouts* and *attenders*. Our calculations showed at least a moderate-sized effect, which might be considered an accomplishment given the compounding problems among the men sent to the programs (e.g., men with heavy alcohol use, previous arrests, and prior long-term abuse). The evidence of a program effect was corroborated by the men's reports about how they avoided violence, the women's attributing the men's change to the program, and an analysis showing deterrence (i.e., perception of sanctions) did not of itself explain program completion or cessation of violence.

Long and Short Programs

My colleagues and I did not, however, find the site effect that we had expected. The outcomes for the longer, more comprehensive programs (i.e., postadjudication, 9 months, additional psychological, alcohol, and women's services) were equivalent to those of the shorter, more streamlined program (i.e., pretrial, 3 months, referral for other problems). The longest program was slightly more likely to have lower rates of severe assault at the 15-month follow-up, but this was countered by equivalent rates of injury and a less-than-significant difference at the 30-month follow-up. These findings persisted even when controlling for possible demographic, personality, and behavioral differences across the sites.

There are several possible reasons for the similar outcomes.

As proponents of *managed care* and *brief therapy* suggest, the streamlined programs appear to be as effective as long-term programs because behavioral change is instigated in the short term. Those who would most benefit from a long-term program, moreover, are very likely to drop out. Another reason could be uniqueness of the programs and their respective contexts. Each program has evolved in response to a different set of resources, personalities, procedures, and norms. For instance, one community has numerous therapists available and a high percentage of batterers familiar with therapy. What we have, then, is not a continuum of intervention systems but a series of exceptional programs.

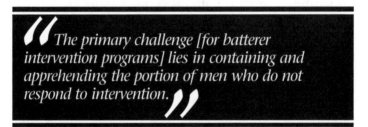

The primary challenge [for batterer intervention programs] lies in containing and apprehending the portion of men who do not respond to intervention.

The reason that makes the most sense to us is the difference in system components across the sites. That is, the system matters. Several problems point to this conclusion:

- The most basic problem may be that the men who would benefit most by long-term counseling are the most likely to drop out.
- A shorter program may be reinforced and enhanced by a swift and certain court response to arrests and subsequent noncompliance.
- Additional services offered by more comprehensive programs may not be sustained with the men who need them the most.
- The women who most need follow-up services and support may not be reached.
- The most dangerous, repeatedly violent men may not be apprehended or sufficiently contained when they reoffend.

All of these shortcomings appeared to be the case.

It was not so much that long-term counseling did not work but that the intervention system of the shorter program compensated for program length. For instance, my colleagues and I found that the pretrial referral got men into the counseling program much more quickly and sent many more men to the program than at the postconviction systems. Periodic court reviews of the referrals ensured quicker and more decisive response to noncompliance and reoffense. The court review dramatically reduced program no-shows and maintained a relatively high completion rate (70%). In sum, the men were held more quickly and decisively accountable for their behavior. . . .

Targets for Improvement

Our multisite evaluation provides some complementary and additional ways to examine the effectiveness of batterer programs. It began with the acknowledgment that batterer programs are fundamentally part of a larger intervention system. To evaluate batterer programs more meaningfully, we may need to account for the system more specifically. Our research team also considered a range of outcomes and examined them over time. The outcomes show a de-escalation and cessation of abuse over time that appeared to have benefited the female partners of the battering men, and batterer counseling appeared to contribute to this result.

The primary challenge lies in containing and apprehending the portion of men who do not respond to intervention. Although identification of these men is difficult at program intake, ongoing monitoring of their behavior after intake could substantially reduce reassault and improve protection. The extent of reassaults shortly after program intake, furthermore, implies a need for more intensive counseling at the beginning. Extending program length in itself does not appear to be the answer without ways to keep the men who need counseling the most from dropping out. More specifically, we recommend swift court action after arrests, screening of major problems, court review of compliance, intensified batterer counseling, and ongoing risk management through male and female case managers, along with conventional batterer counseling. Some administrative expertise and modest funding are needed to achieve and implement these sorts of recommendations, however.

Our recommendations for program structure and system development coincide with precedents in the sexual assault field. Despite earlier analysis suggesting ineffective sex offender counseling, recent reviews of the research found evidence for effectiveness of these programs. Those working in this field attribute the success to the shift toward cognitive-behavioral counseling—similar to the approach used in conventional batterer counseling. The other notable component is the community supervision of and response to sex offenders.

We are . . . sending a message that men can and must change their behavior toward women.

Sex offender program staff usually work very closely with probation and parole officers to monitor and supervise these offenders. They monitor the offenders' use of avoidance techniques, pornography, "cruising" locations, and alcohol. Furthermore, all states now have registries of convicted sex offenders, which include information about the offenders' strategies and victims. They also notify communities about the residence of convicted sex offenders. The registries and notification heighten informal surveillance by neighbors and by police. In sum, the combination of cognitive-behavior counseling and a coordinated community response appear to have an impact.

Need for Community Involvement

Our recommendations point to a broader goal of community development. In the process, they may be taking us back to our starting point. Battered-women's advocates began women's shelters and services and accepted the advent of batterer-counseling programs out of a larger vision of social change. Their goal was to help individual women directly and also to reform community agencies, increase public awareness, and promote justice for women in the courts. Ideally, it was to bring a greater safety, peace, equality, and appreciation for women. The current appeals for coordinated community response in everything from community policing to domestic violence also corroborate our recommendations. Coordinated community response requires a kind of community development that brings agencies together and helps reform them along the way. More people become involved in the intervention efforts and more become aware and concerned. New funding and demonstration projects for this kind of community development show promise, but will need evaluation of their own for fine-tuning and further development.

One can take heart that the early initiatives have carried us this far and turned into concrete strategies for broadened intervention. The current interventions do appear to be making some difference for the women most in need of relief. The main challenge appears to be in making the existing components of intervention work together more decisively and consistently. They need to hold men accountable for their behavior. According to our multisite evaluation, the notion of *accountability*, so frequently urged in batterer counseling, warrants some reinforcement. More has to be done, on many levels—in schools, in the workplace, in the culture, in the hearts of men. Batterer counseling has been a kind of laboratory for this ultimate work. By trying to contain, change, and help some of the most resistant and severe offenders, we are finding ways to affect other men in other places. We are also sending a message that men can and must change their behavior toward women. For these and many other reasons, batterer counseling deserves to be continued but with more attention to the intervention system as a whole.

7

Batterer Intervention Programs Do Not Prevent Domestic Violence

Shelly Jackson

Shelly Jackson is a program manager in the office of research and evaluation at the National Institute of Justice, part of the U.S. Department of Justice's Office of Justice Programs.

Men convicted of domestic abuse are often required to attend batterer intervention programs instead of, or in addition to, serving jail time. However, recent research casts doubt on whether these programs actually help to prevent further abuse. Evaluation of two programs found little change in behavior and no change in attitude in men who had gone through the programs. Other types of batterer intervention programs have been less thoroughly evaluated, but their effectiveness is also in doubt. Intervention programs can suffer from a variety of flaws, including being based on inaccurate assumptions and lacking sensitivity to different cultures. Batterer intervention programs should not be abandoned, but depending on them to protect women or devoting large amounts of resources to them is inadvisable when there is so little evidence that they really work. Programs, implementation, and evaluation techniques all need to be improved before these programs can be considered an effective response to domestic violence.

Shelly Jackson, "Batterer Intervention Programs: Where Do We Go from Here?" National Institute of Justice Special Report, June 2003.

With the establishment of proarrest policies in the 1980s, increasing numbers of batterers were seen in criminal courts across the country. Initially, they were sentenced to jail. Some victims, however, began to say that although they wanted the battering to stop, they did not want their partners incarcerated. To respond to these requests while still holding batterers accountable, offenders were referred to batterer intervention programs (BIPs, also known as spouse abuse abatement programs or SAAPs). This has led researchers and advocates to ask, "Do these programs work?"

Although early evaluations suggested that BIPs reduce battering, recent evaluations based on more rigorous designs find little or no reduction. The methodological limitations of virtually all these evaluations, however, make it impossible to say how effective BIPs are.

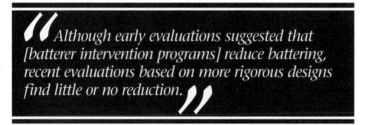

Although early evaluations suggested that [batterer intervention programs] reduce battering, recent evaluations based on more rigorous designs find little or no reduction.

This NIJ [National Institute of Justice] Special Report describes the results of two recent evaluations that add to this growing literature. Lynette Feder and David Forde in Broward County, Florida, and Robert Davis, Bruce Taylor, and Christopher Maxwell in Brooklyn, New York, conducted experimental evaluations of programs based on the Duluth model [the Duluth Domestic Abuse Intervention Project, developed by Minnesota Program Development, Inc.]. The Brooklyn evaluation found some reductions in battering, but it found no evidence that the program had any effect on batterers' attitudes. The Broward County evaluation found no change in either behavior or attitudes. . . .

Types of Batterer Intervention Programs

The first BIP models were psychoeducational programs. One such program, the Duluth model, is based on the feminist theory that patriarchal ideology, which encourages men to control their partners, causes domestic violence. The Duluth model helps men confront their attitudes about control and teaches them other strategies for dealing with their partners. This model is the most common form of BIP in the Nation; many States mandate that BIPs conform to the Duluth model.

There are several alternatives to the Duluth model. Cognitive-behavioral intervention views battering as a result of errors in thinking and focuses on skills training and anger management. Another model, group practice, works from the premise that battering has multiple causes and therefore combines a psychoeducational curriculum, cognitive-behavioral techniques, and an assessment of individual needs. Examples of these programs include Emerge and AMEND (Abusive Men Exploring New Directions).

Programs based on batterer typologies or profiles—most commonly psychological and criminal-justice-based typologies—are gaining popularity. BIPs based on these profiles are just beginning to be developed and have not been evaluated.

Another, more controversial, intervention is couples therapy. This model views men and women as equal participants in creating disturbances in the relationship. Although couples therapy may be appropriate for some people, it is widely criticized for inappropriately assigning the woman a share of the blame for the continuation of violence.

Evaluation of Batterer Intervention Programs

More than 35 BIP evaluations have been published. Early studies, which used quasi-experimental designs, consistently found small program effects; when more methodologically rigorous evaluations were undertaken, the results were inconsistent and disappointing. Most of the later studies found that treatment effects were limited to a small reduction in reoffending, although evidence indicates that for most participants (perhaps those already motivated to change), BIPs may end the most violent and threatening behaviors. The results, however, remain inconclusive because of methodological flaws in these evaluations.

Although most of the programs evaluated followed the Duluth model, cognitive-behavior therapy has also been examined. In 21 of 24 controlled studies, reoffense rates were lower among program participants than among the control group (although not all differences were statistically significant). These effects were larger in demonstration programs (implemented by a researcher) than in practical programs (implemented by a juvenile or criminal justice agency) or a combination of the two. This suggests that the way a program is put into practice (i.e., how faithful it is to the intervention model) may be key in determining its impact. Outcomes were measured only for an average of 20 weeks after the end of treatment, which did not allow an assessment of longer term reoffense rates.

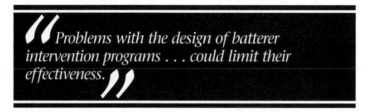

Problems with the design of batterer intervention programs . . . could limit their effectiveness.

Differences in evaluation methods account for much of the inconsistency in findings. Pure experimental designs, favored by researchers because of their methodological rigor, make finding true effects easier and reduce the likelihood of error but are challenging to carry out in the field; as a result, design flaws may cast doubt on the results. Quasi-experimental designs, which differ from pure experiments in that group assignment is not random, are easier to carry out but are more open to misinterpretation. Thus, it is hard to tell whether program effects are true or masked because the evaluation was compromised in the field.

The . . . BIP evaluations in Broward County, Florida, and Brooklyn, New York, . . . used classical experimental designs: Batterers were randomly assigned to experimental or control groups. In Broward County, men in the experimental group were sentenced to 1 year of probation and 26 weeks of group counseling at a BIP, whereas men in the control group were sentenced to 1 year of probation. In Brooklyn . . . some men in the experimental group received their treatment in 26 weekly sessions, while others attended longer, twice-weekly sessions for 8 weeks. Men assigned to the control group took part in a community service program. In both studies, the two groups were tested to see whether treatment had changed their attitudes toward violence. Recidivism was measured both by official measures and by victim reports of abuse. In Broward County, offender self-reports of abuse were also recorded.

The Broward County study found no significant difference between the experimental and control groups in attitudes toward the role of women, whether wife beating should be a crime, or whether the State had the right to intervene in cases of domestic violence. It also found no significant difference between groups in victims' perceptions of the likelihood that their partners would beat them again. Official measures followed the same pattern: No significant difference was found between groups in violations of probation or rearrests. In fact, men assigned to the experimental group were more likely to be rearrested than members of the control group unless they had attended all of the treatment sessions.

In the Brooklyn study, initial findings showed that the experimental group as a whole was less likely than the control group to be arrested again for a crime against the same victim. On a closer look, however, only the 26-week group had significantly fewer official complaints than the control group at 6 and 12 months. The pattern of victim reports was the same (although the differences between the 8- and 26-week groups were not statistically significant). The study found no difference among the three groups in attitudes toward domestic violence.

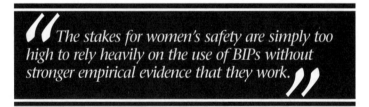

The stakes for women's safety are simply too high to rely heavily on the use of BIPs without stronger empirical evidence that they work.

These studies, however, suffer from several limitations. Response rates were low and sample attrition high in both studies. The measures of batterers' attitudes toward domestic violence and likelihood to engage in further abuse are of questionable validity. Random assignment to the control group was overridden to a significant extent, especially in the Brooklyn study. Without process evaluations, there is no way to tell how well the Duluth model was being implemented in the treatment sites. . . .

Program Design Problems

In addition to these methodological problems, problems with the design of BIPs themselves could limit their effectiveness.

Program models are sometimes not carried out completely. Testing how faithful programs are to the models on which they are based requires process evaluations, which, to date, few evaluations have incorporated.

BIP designs also may have conceptual limitations. The Duluth model assumes that all batterers seek to control their partners. Batterers' motivations for violence may differ, so the same type of intervention may not work with all batterers.

BIPs also may be limited by their lack of cultural specificity. Although domestic violence occurs in all populations, treatment approaches may need to be tailored to serve specific populations. It may be unreasonable to expect Duluth-model interventions based on white feminist theory to work effectively with minority populations. Not everyone agrees with this proposition, however. The House of Ruth in Baltimore, Maryland, deliberately created an ethnically integrated group treatment setting based on the Duluth model to stress that domestic violence has nothing to do with race or socioeconomic status. In the early 2000s, NIJ funded an experimental evaluation to examine whether a batterer intervention model designed specifically for black men is more effective for them than an integrated model.

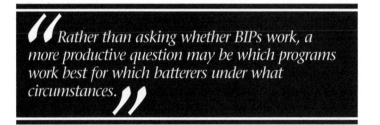

Rather than asking whether BIPs work, a more productive question may be which programs work best for which batterers under what circumstances.

Although this is changing, few interventions to date have assessed abusers' mental health and substance abuse treatment needs. These factors do not excuse the battering, but they may make interventions less effective. Including more services, however, may have the unintended effect of increasing the length of a program, its associated costs, and possibly its dropout rates. It is unclear which is more effective: keeping program length to a minimum or adding components (and thereby lengthening the program). These factors deserve more research.

Programs may remain minimally effective until they consider the batterer's readiness to change. Theories focusing on understanding the stages of personal change suggest that the batterer will change his behavior only when he is ready to change. Thus, mandating treatment for batterers who are not ready to change may be ineffective. BIPs may be effective for batterers who are ready to change, but batterers who are not yet ready may require other interventions.

Policy Questions

Although interventions are proliferating, there is little evidence that they work. This raises important policy questions:

- Do batterer intervention programs waste valuable resources?
- Do they create a false sense of security in women who are led to believe that their batterer will reform?
- Is it prudent to mandate batterers to BIPs when there is little evidence that they work?

Unfortunately, the latest contributions to this growing literature cannot answer these questions and raise additional issues. Although the Brooklyn study found some differences between those who completed the 8-week program, those who completed the 26-week program, and those who attended no program, it remains unclear whether these differences were due to a program effect or a monitoring effect. Further research is needed to clarify this issue.

One thing is clear: Rigorous evaluations are essential to answering the pressing questions about what works and using that knowledge to influence public policy. The stakes for women's safety are simply too high to rely heavily on the use of BIPs without stronger empirical evidence that they work.

Are these evaluations accurate in saying that BIPs are not very effective at changing batterers' behaviors and attitudes, or are the small program effects merely the result of methodological shortcomings in the evaluations themselves that mask program effectiveness? Both issues may need to be addressed. To enhance our knowledge, both BIPs and evaluations likely will have to be improved.

Improving Program Evaluations

Over the years, the quality of BIP evaluation has improved steadily, but several barriers remain to be addressed. Although a variety of designs have been used to study BIPs (e.g., pre-post, quasi-experimental, and experimental designs), most researchers still consider the experiment to be the best evaluation method. Experimental designs are difficult to carry out in court settings; the pressures involved reduce many experimental evaluations to quasi-experiments that cannot deliver the necessary knowledge. Researchers, practitioners, and policymakers must work together to develop strategies that enable experimental evaluations to be carried out vigorously. All BIP evaluations, regardless of design, face difficulties in interviewing batterers and victims during the follow-up period. Researchers will need to find innovative ways to maintain contact with batterers and victims over time. Researchers also will need to develop reliable and valid outcome measures rather than relying solely on official records such as rearrests and probation violations to validate batterer and victim reports. . . .

Improving Intervention Programs

In addition to improving the quality of the experimental design and results, improvements in the concepts underlying the various models of BIPs may be warranted. New intervention approaches could be developed based on theories derived from existing research into the causes of battering. Useful research has been conducted on batterer profiles, and new treatment approaches are being designed to match those profiles with appropriate interventions. Although this approach still must be tested, it may prove more productive than a one-size-fits-all approach. It also may be advantageous for researchers to draw lessons from other disciplines, such as substance abuse interventions.

BIPs may be effective only in the context of broader criminal justice innovations. It may be helpful to see interventions as part of a broader criminal justice and community response to domestic violence that includes arrest, restraining orders, intensive monitoring of batterers, and changes to social norms that may inadvertently tolerate partner violence. If monitoring is in part responsible for lower reoffense rates, as the Brooklyn experiment suggests, judicial monitoring may be particularly effective. The Judicial Oversight Demonstration initiative, a collaboration of NIJ, the Violence Against Women Office, and three local jurisdictions, is testing this proposition. Other innovations might include mandatory intervention until a committee determines that the batterer is no longer a danger to his partner (i.e., indeterminate probation and intervention), an approach that has been used with sex offenders. Improvements in the ways BIPs are put into practice may also be necessary, as variations in how programs are carried out may reduce program effectiveness. Some programs have few sanctions for dropping out, whereas others closely monitor batterer attendance. This suggests the need to test the effectiveness of close monitoring and required attendance. Consistent with dose-response theory, batterers should be exposed to the entire program before outcome measures are taken. Drug treatment research has shown that length of treatment (i.e., dosage) influences the outcome. One way to determine whether a program is being carried out as designed is to conduct process and impact evaluations at the same time to understand how program implementation affects the impact evaluation.

The field of batterer intervention is still in its infancy, and much remains to be learned. Rather than asking whether BIPs work, a more productive question may be which programs work best for which batterers under which circumstances, a decidedly more complex question. If this approach is adopted, improved theories of battering will need to precede new responses that will need to be tested. If differential sentencing is incorporated into the criminal justice system, procedures will need to be developed to ensure that it is carried out fairly. As BIPs are a relatively new response to a critical social problem, it is too early to abandon the concept. It is also too early to believe that we have all the answers. Research and evaluation supported by NIJ will continue to add to our growing knowledge of responses to battering, including batterer intervention programs.

8

Community Involvement Helps Prevent Domestic Violence

P. Catlin Fullwood

P. Catlin Fullwood is the organizer of the Community Engagement for Change Initiative, a project of the Family Violence Prevention Fund in San Francisco, California.

Programs to prevent or reduce domestic violence should involve not just the criminal justice and child welfare systems but the entire community. Some pioneering programs are beginning to enlist whole communities in combating domestic violence. The most successful projects raise awareness of the problem and help community residents find the services they need, including shelters and counseling. Effective programs also build networks of leaders who will work to end violence. The best programs take into account and respect the culture of the communities in which they are presented. These programs involve local people at every step of the process, recognizing that the social changes needed to eliminate domestic violence must be developed by those who live in the communities where violence occurs rather than being imposed from the outside.

For years, child welfare workers and domestic violence advocates have noted that child abuse and domestic violence—

P. Catlin Fullwood. This material was adapted from the publication entitled *Preventing Family Violence: Community Engagement Makes the Difference,* September 2002. Produced by the Family Violence Prevention Fund. Copyright © 2002 by the Family Violence Prevention Fund.

together referred to as family violence—often occur in the same families. Although numerous programs address these two problems separately, few have looked at them together. Yet family violence can have devastating consequences on individuals, families and the communities where they live.

Nearly one-third of American women report being physically or sexually abused by a husband or boyfriend at some point in their lives. Reports of child abuse or maltreatment are equally alarming, with almost one million confirmed reports of abused or neglected children in 1998. In that same year, an estimated 1,100 children (three per day) died of abuse or neglect, nearly 80 percent of them children under five years of age.

Child abuse and domestic violence are so intertwined that a 1995 report by the U.S. Advisory Board on Child Abuse and Neglect suggested that domestic violence may be the single major precursor to child abuse and neglect fatalities in this country. In Oregon, for example, a 1993 study showed that domestic violence occurred in 41 percent of the families in which children had been critically injured or killed. In a 1994 study of 200 substantiated child abuse cases, the Massachusetts Department of Social Services found mention of domestic violence in 48 percent of the cases.

Most institutional response to family violence is based in the child welfare and criminal justice systems. In the past, it was rare for child protection and domestic violence workers to coordinate their efforts or work together. In fact, there was often tension between the two. Child protection workers, with a government-based mandate, advocated for safety of children and preservation of the family unit when possible. Domestic violence workers, on the other hand, grew from a community-based movement aimed at protecting women from their batterers and focused on efforts to help women leave abusive relationships. They did not collaborate with one another, and they rarely worked with members of the communities they served to develop family violence prevention strategies.

Why Involving the Community Is Important

While appropriate services and responsive institutions are important components in the effort to counter family violence, it takes more than that to generate and sustain real change. But those who are most affected by the violence—the families and communities that live with it—have largely been left out of discussions about the solutions. Yet they are the ones who know all too well how violence affects their daily lives, their environment, their relationships, and their ability to move freely in their neighborhoods and among their peers.

> *Those who are most affected by [domestic] violence—the families and communities that live with it—have largely been left out of discussions about the solutions.*

Families and community members play a crucial role in preventing family violence for many reasons:

- Studies show that abused women turn first to those closest to them—extended family, friends, and neighbors—before they reach out to an organization or professional service provider. Relatively few access shelter services. And they seek out government institutions—police, courts, and child protection agencies—last.
- Families that experience violence are often disconnected from traditional service providers and isolated from services offered outside their immediate neighborhood.
- Community members often know which families need help and which services can make a difference.
- Community members know the cultural values, traditions, and practices that support violence—as well as those that can be used appropriately to intervene and stop it.
- Communities include men, women, and youth who understand the connection between violence in the home and on the street and see family violence as a primary barrier to community development and revitalization.
- Most community residents and leaders have the willingness and capacity to develop the skills needed to conduct family violence prevention and intervention activities.

Examining Community Programs

The community is thus a critical place to hold the conversation about preventing and stopping family violence. Yet little is known about how to engage local community leaders and residents around these issues. A few organizations, foundations, and agencies are beginning to look at the link between child abuse and domestic violence, but programs that address them together are still, for the most part, in their infancy. The Family Violence Prevention Fund (FVPF) launched the Community Engagement for Change Initiative in order to identify and learn from organizations and systems that are employing community mobilization strategies to prevent family violence.

The FVPF visited a range of community-based programs engaged in local mobilization efforts to prevent and reduce family violence. These programs, located all across the country, operate in specific neighborhoods or with constituency groups connected by affinity or race. Participants define family violence broadly, including child abuse and maltreatment, domestic violence, dating violence, sexual assault, and same-sex violence between intimate partners. In some of the organizations, child abuse was the original focus, in others it was domestic violence. In a few, substance abuse, youth violence, HIV or community violence was the introductory factor; and in a few others, the starting point was a community development approach. But wherever they started, the community organizations surveyed have come to understand the connections between the various forms of family violence and other problems affecting their community.

> *The pioneering programs [engaging communities in domestic violence prevention] . . . are learning from the ground up.*

All of the programs are using a community engagement strategy, defined as "bringing together the talents, resources and skills of people in the community in order to increase their collective power and work for social change"—in this case, decreasing family violence. The pioneering programs surveyed by the FVPF are learning from the ground up, using community-based engagement strategies to reach out to families that need help and to involve local leaders, residents, service providers, and government institutions in stopping violence. They all share a commitment to listen to the community and to learn from the families they serve. They are all working to connect families to appropriate services. And they are all grappling with the complexities of focusing on family violence in communities struggling with various degrees of poverty, economic hardship, educational disadvantages, and substance abuse. The task is a challenging one.

Their ultimate goal, however, is quite clear: to prevent and reduce family violence. Few have developed ways of measuring their progress. They realize that dealing with ongoing and interconnecting problems means there are no "quick fixes"; they must stay in it for the long haul. But they already have a lot of stories to tell and lessons to share. . . .

Characteristics of Successful Programs

The FVPF's study found no simple solutions to family violence or proven practices to end it. The organizations surveyed take different approaches and bring different experiences and services to the table. But all of them look at the problem of family violence in the context of the conditions present in the community. This means finding and building on community assets, using culturally appropriate messages and services, and cultivating and supporting local leaders who can advocate for and sustain change. The five main goals discussed here are intertwined, and most of the organizations work on several of them simultaneously.

What It Takes to Prevent Family Violence in the Community
1. Raising awareness of the problem of family violence and establishing social norms that make violence unacceptable.
2. Connecting community residents to services.
3. Changing social and community conditions that contribute to violence.
4. Building networks of leaders within a community.
5. Making services and institutions accountable to community needs. . . .

Guidelines for Working with Communities

The site visits and interviews with each of the programs, their leaders and community residents yielded a number of guidelines for working with, and within, communities to prevent family violence. These practical tips cover coalition building, collaboration, recognition of cultural values, communication and more. They reflect the real complexity of the work the organizations are undertaking, in environments that often include significant poverty, unemployment, and substance abuse, in addition to family violence. Recommendations include:

- *Help community members see family violence as a priority.* Community members have many issues on their mind. They may be more willing to begin with a discussion about drug dealers and violence on the streets than to talk about violence in households, which is often seen as a private issue. But once families sense "permission" to speak out and know they can do so safely, they will begin to make powerful connections between violence in the home and other problems plaguing the community. Organizers can provide a safe forum where people can talk about the impact of family violence on the community as a whole—in terms of the safety and well-being of everyone, the link between violence at home and on the street, the incarceration of perpetrators, the resultant increase in poverty and children growing up without a father in the home, the dangers of domestic violence if it spills over into public realms such as the workplace, etc.

> *Efforts to address child abuse and domestic violence need to be compatible with cultural mores.*

- *Help residents and local organizers address family violence issues in ways that do not stigmatize or label people as "abused" or "abusers."* This will help promote community norms that make it acceptable to talk about family violence and thus to intervene when someone is in danger.
- *"Invite, don't indict" the men in the community.* Men often feel blamed, defensive and excluded when the issue of family violence comes up. Some believe that social service systems are biased in favor of women and punitive to men, particularly poor men of color. Framing all men as perpetrators or potential perpetrators makes it difficult to bring them into the conversation. It is important to create a language and context for community mobilization that includes and welcomes men and to recognize that they may be the most effective carriers of anti-

violence messages to other men and boys.

- *Remember that the real work of community mobilization happens within the cultural context of a community.* Efforts to address child abuse and domestic violence need to be compatible with cultural mores and a long-standing need to protect the community from external forces that may be perceived as hostile. When shaping program goals and methods, listen to the community's voices, which reflect its cultural attitudes and traditions. Programs created from a distance by outsiders have less chance of success.

> *Violence occurs at the local level. And that is where the shift [to prevention] has to happen.*

- *Help residents identify new community-driven ways of holding perpetrators accountable for ending their abuse. Devise strategies that do not rely so heavily on the criminal justice or child welfare systems.* Forcing communities to air issues that may open them to unwelcome social services or criminal justice sanctions can provoke resistance or even hostility. This is especially true when workable solutions are not offered. In communities of color and immigrant communities, for example, calling the police may not be seen as a viable option by many abuse survivors who fear that law enforcement could result in incarceration, deportation, or placement of their children in foster care. Among lesbians and gay men, where the perpetrator and victim are of the same sex, and the community is often small, issues are especially complex. It is essential for a community to determine how to hold perpetrators of violence accountable for stopping their violence in ways that take into account the real or perceived barriers to disclosure and intervention.
- *Integrate activities about family violence into the regular life of the community.* Talk about family violence at community events such as health fairs, block parties, back-to-school picnics, English-as-a-Second-Language classes, etc.
- *Build individual capacity to intervene with friends and families.* Empowering individuals with the information, tools and resources they need to help victims and perpetrators

of abuse is a critical component of any community engagement effort. As victims and perpetrators feel safe enough to disclose their abuse, it is important that organizers know how to respond appropriately and where to refer them for help.

- *Close the gap between social service providers and the communities they serve.* Institutions can be involved in community efforts to stop family violence in a variety of ways, including lending resources and support or basing workers in the neighborhood. Providers who are involved at this level are more likely to learn what families need and to adapt their programs accordingly.
- *Understand that people listen to those they trust.* This trust can be based on common background or shared past experiences or it can grow from working together. In engaging a community, involve existing community structures or leaders who are already trusted. Be a consistent and ongoing presence. Community members are justifiably wary of initiatives designed to solve the latest "problem" that has been "discovered" by outsiders.

Local Efforts Lead to Long-Term Change

Community engagement to end family violence is complex work, but changing society happens in small increments, one family, one step at a time. . . . Family violence does not occur in a vacuum and . . . community solutions must reflect the full scope of issues of concern to their residents. Working in partnership with residents can push advocates of social change to come up with new and creative approaches as they discover ways to help create healthy communities where people want to live: where there are jobs, a connection of spirit, where families know when and how to get help.

Violence occurs at the local level. And that is where the shift has to happen—and where it has to be sustained over time. The most promising of the community projects surveyed by the FVPF involve local residents at every step of the process, from identifying the problem and spreading the word to developing interventions and implementing strategies for change. The organizations that do this kind of work recognize the sense of ownership that grows when community members are involved in solving problems. They also recognize the importance of collaborating with the systems charged with responding to family violence—and of holding those systems accountable for changing practices.

It requires a great deal of time, resources and patience to engage in a community-based process to address child abuse and domestic violence at the same time, but the potential benefits are tremendous. When solutions come from within, the changes that result are long-term and truly reflect a community's resources, culture, needs and goals.

9

Men Can Play an Important Role in Preventing Domestic Violence

Denis Devine

Denis Devine is a staff writer at the North County Times, *a newspaper published in San Diego and Riverside counties, California.*

Most men never batter women, but that does not mean that domestic violence is "not their problem." On the contrary, men who respect women need to take an active role in preventing domestic violence by showing other men that disrespect, whether in the form of actual battering or sexist jokes, is wrong. Thoughtful men need to counter common beliefs such as the idea that showing or discussing feelings is "unmanly" or that manhood is proved through control of women. It is especially important to teach boys and young men more peaceful definitions of manhood and of conflict resolution. Men who recognize that domestic violence is a men's as well as a women's issue can take a number of steps to prevent or reduce violence in their communities.

I've never beaten my girlfriend, or struck my mom or sisters. Most men reading this can say the same. So it's easy to think of violence against women as a terrible social problem, perhaps, a rampant injustice, a public health threat, but most of all, someone else's problem. If a particularly tragic tale of domestic violence tugged at my conscience, I had imagined the most I could do was donate to a shelter for abuse victims.

But on Monday, Valentine's Day [2005], I heard a large group of compassionate, bold men say something different: violence against women is something all men must deal with. Because it's mostly males doing it—93 percent of violence against female adult victims is committed by men—the responsibility falls upon us to stop it. And that means far more than calling the cops when we hear a crime in progress.

It means teaching young men that disrespecting women is not manly or acceptable, but that talking about their feelings is. It means letting friends who tell sexist jokes know that we don't find it funny. It means exploring the ways our own behavior contributes to an atmosphere of sexism and machismo that teaches women they are less than men, and that we will enforce that dominance with our fists, if need be.

While most men chose chocolate, flowers and jewels for their lady loves on Valentine's Day, a group of about 200 men and women from the San Diego County [California] region gathered in a Mission Bay conference center to discuss how to help stop gender-based violence—another way of saying violence against women like our mothers, sisters, daughters and girlfriends.

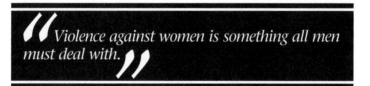

Violence against women is something all men must deal with.

"It's just not a problem on most men's radar. It's not a big deal to them," said Steve Allen, cofounder of the Men's Leadership Forum, the committee of the San Diego Domestic Violence Council that organized the conference. "We're saying it is a big deal. We're saying if you knew the societal cost, let alone the human tragedy, it would be a big deal."

In North County, one such tragedy reached a conclusion . . . [in early February 2005]. Eugene Orange was sentenced to 111 years for brutally murdering his wife, Zeda Barnett, a 37-year-old mother of three boys.

Barnett had twice sought temporary restraining orders against her husband in the months before her murder. On her second application, the well-loved Palomar College employee wrote in July 2003 about what happened when she told Orange she wanted to end their relationship: "He got very angry and stated to me that 'our marriage is not over' and that if he cannot have me 'no one can.'" Before that month was over, Orange fulfilled his deadly threat, stabbing his wife to death in their Escondido apartment.

Many people had warning that tragedy was coming. The Men's Leadership Forum seeks to educate men who might find themselves in those shoes—either striking their wives or learning that their friends do—so that we can prevent more suffering and pain like what Eugene Orange rained down upon Zeda Barnett.

Domestic Violence Is a Men's Issue

For too long, violence against women has been mischaracterized as a "women's issue." When a newspaper story broaches the subject, guys often flip toward the sports pages—only to routinely encounter stories about athletes raping, abusing and otherwise mistreating women.

Don McPherson, the forum's keynote speaker, railed against the way boys are taught not to cry, express their emotions or "throw like a girl"—a particularly nasty slur to a child who grew up to become an NFL quarterback. McPherson—whose Sports Leadership Institute challenges sports to fulfill its promise of teaching children how to be healthy adults—criticized the narrow definitions that confine manhood to notions like strength, control and hiding emotions.

"Where are the opportunities for men to express their other characteristics?" he asked. "The answer is to raise boys to be whole people. My friends kid me about 'getting in touch with my feminine side,' but that's not what I'm talking about. I'm talking about getting in touch with my wholeness."

The men leading [the Valentine's Day] . . . workshops emphasized that the lessons boys learn about manhood sabotage their ability to handle relationship stress later in life, which leads many to turn to violence to resolve conflicts with lovers and others.

McPherson isn't the only jock working to stop violence against women: In a televised address about his Safe at Home Foundation, New York Yankees manager Joe Torre revealed the emotional scars left by his father's abuse of his mother.

Torre's story echoed what Zeda Barnett's 16-year-old son, Kyrell, told a judge Feb. 10 [2005]: "I'm really mad that my mom is gone," Kyrell said at his stepfather's sentencing. "Ever since he came into my life, my life has been a living hell."

Act Locally Against a Global Problem

The Men's Leadership Forum seeks to address what experts say is a global pandemic of violence against women by encouraging men to act locally—in their homes and communities, among their families and friends.

The men gathered [at the San Diego conference] . . . were social workers, high school guidance counselors, sports coaches, pastors, fathers, sons, brothers, husbands. They were all sick of the war on women that men have been waging.

The San Diego County Health and Human Services Agency's Office of Violence Prevention reports:
- In 2003, law enforcement officers reported 21,272 domestic violence incidents in the county, including 3,207 in the north coastal region and 2,361 in the north inland.
- About 21 out of every 1,000 households in San Diego County reported a domestic violence incident in 2003.

According to the U.S. Department of Justice's National Crime Victimization Survey:
- More than 2.5 million American women experience violence each year.
- About one-third of female victims suffer injuries as a result of the crime.

According to the National Violence Against Women Survey:
- 25 percent of women reported suffering violence at the hands of an intimate partner over the course of their lives, compared with 8 percent of men.
- The more serious the violence, the greater the disparity in the victims' gender. If it really hurts, it's more likely a woman at the receiving end.
- 76 percent of women victims reported being assaulted or raped by past or present intimate partners.

Men are committing the overwhelming majority of violence—especially violence against women and girls—but that doesn't mean most men are violent toward women. Of the minority who are hurting women, most aren't sociopaths or psychopaths.

Instead, as Jackson Katz, one of the movement's forefathers, put it in a 2003 paper, they are "men who have learned to use force to maintain power and control over women, children or other men to 'prove their manhood,' or to try to get their emotional or physical needs met."

Helping Other Men Change

That cruel curriculum—lessons that hurt both men and women, but women more—was at the heart of [the San Diego] conference.

Workshops sliced off various portions of gender-based violence's poisoned apple: the limits of law enforcement's ability to respond, the effects on children, discrepancies in how men and women communicate, how religious communities can help, and how concepts of masculinity contribute to the problem.

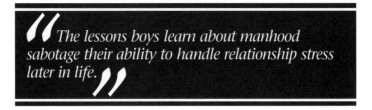

The lessons boys learn about manhood sabotage their ability to handle relationship stress later in life.

Men swapped strategies for dealing with everything from sexist jokes told by friends to neighbors who abuse their wives. It was a common theme: It's time for men who get it to speak up and let other men know they don't approve, becoming what Katz calls "empowered bystanders."

"A lot of guys think it's OK to do this sort of thing to women because no one has appropriately challenged them on it," said Allen, the director of legal services for the San Diego-based Center for Community Solutions. "A joke can just not be funny, it can be outright offensive, but men don't appropriately confront this guy, because we don't want to seem wimpy and sissy."

Allen added, "These poor guys, it's hard to have sympathy for them, but they learned it, and we want to help them unlearn it. This effort is also going to benefit men. There are thousands and thousands of guys currently incarcerated for domestic violence and sexual assault because they didn't have alternatives, they didn't know better."

David Wexler, executive director of the San Diego-based Relationship Training Institute, recently returned from a guest spot on the "Dr. Phil" show, where he discussed his new book, *When Good Men Behave Badly: Change Your Behavior, Change Your Relationship*. His institute has helped thousands of service members and their families through the U.S. Navy Family Advocacy Center in San Diego.

Wexler dissected . . . the many ways in which the lessons young men learn about manhood cripple their ability to communicate emotions later in life or handle stresses that arise in intimate relationships. Wexler acknowledged the truly "bad" men that won't make good partners for women under any circumstances. But, he said, "most men who mess up in relationships get tripped up by the emotional demands" but can learn how to handle stress without resorting to violence.

For the men who already know how to resolve conflicts peacefully, express their emotions and appreciate a more complex idea of masculinity, Wexler said, "It's the good guys' job to bring the guys in the middle over to our side."

Too often, a man's first exposure to the ideas discussed [at the conference] . . . comes when a judge orders him to attend a counseling group for batterers; several therapists who organize such groups throughout San Diego County were in attendance.

Doug Willford hopes men and women don't wait that long to come to the discussion groups he leads at the Life Skills Learning Center in San Marcos.

"It's difficult to get people to get help before they get in trouble," he said. "Sometimes we don't know how we'll react until we experience severe stress. It's better to get help now rather than waiting."

Spiritual Aspects

Also moving to help are five San Diego County congregations, including St. Peter's Roman Catholic Church in Fallbrook.

These religious groups, behind the leadership of the Diocese of San Diego, are participating in the Safe Place Faith Communities Program. That means St. Peter's is building a set of resources—a team of trained volunteers, a network of resources, a safe place to talk—for its parishioners who want help with domestic violence.

"We want to take away the fear, shame and negativity of talking to people about it," said Terry Hawthorne, pastoral associate at St. Peter's. While the parish already hosts a weekly visit by a bilingual domestic violence counselor from the Palomar Pomerado Health System and has an active Men's Group, the Safe Place program will coordinate the church's ability to respond to parishioners in spiritual crisis—the hell of family violence, hell for the victims and torment for the perpetrators, too.

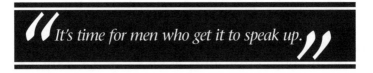

It's time for men who get it to speak up.

"There is a spiritual aspect to this," Hawthorne said. "People might start to believe that they are unlovable by God, by other people, and their self-esteem goes really down. They need to know that the church is there for them in this and in all things in which they need help."

All this work might not be able to stop every Eugene Orange in North County from beating or even killing his spouse, but we must try. For there are children, boys and girls, who are watching, and counting on us to make a stand. That stand might not require the dramatic rescue men love to imagine; it might merely require us to examine our behavior and make a subtle but significant change.

What Men Can Do to Prevent Gender Violence

1. Approach gender violence as a men's issue involving men of all ages and socioeconomic, racial and ethnic backgrounds. View men not only as perpetrators or possible offenders, but as empowered bystanders who can confront abusive peers.
2. If someone you know is abusing his female partner—or is disrespectful or abusive to girls and women in general—don't look the other way. If you feel comfortable doing so, try to talk to him about it. Urge him to seek help. Or if you don't know what to do, consult a friend, a parent, a professor or a counselor. Don't remain silent.
3. Have the courage to look inward. Question your own attitudes. Don't be defensive when something you do or say ends up hurting someone else. Try hard to understand how your own attitudes and actions might inadvertently perpetuate sexism and violence, and work toward changing them.

4. If you suspect that a woman close to you is being abused or has been sexually assaulted, gently ask if you can help.

5. If you are emotionally, psychologically, physically or sexually abusive to women, or have been in the past, seek professional help now.

6. Be an ally to women who are working to end all forms of gender violence. Support the work of campus-based women's centers. Attend "Take Back the Night" rallies and other public events. Raise money for community-based rape crisis centers and battered women's shelters. If you belong to a team or fraternity, or another student group, organize a fund-raiser.

7. Recognize and speak out against homophobia and gay-bashing. Discrimination and violence against lesbians and gays are wrong in and of themselves. This abuse also has direct links to sexism (e.g., the sexual orientation of men who speak out against sexism is often questioned, a conscious or unconscious strategy intended to silence them. This is a key reason few men do so.).

8. Attend programs, take courses, watch films and read articles and books about multicultural masculinities, gender inequality and the root causes of gender violence. Educate yourself and others about how larger social forces affect the conflicts between individual men and women.

9. Don't fund sexism. Refuse to purchase any magazine, rent any video, subscribe to any Web site or buy any music that portrays girls or women in a sexually degrading or abusive manner. Protest sexism in the media.

10. Mentor and teach young boys about how to be men in ways that don't involve degrading or abusing girls and women. Volunteer to work with gender violence prevention programs, including anti-sexist men's programs. Lead by example.

10

Educational Programs Aid in Preventing Domestic Violence

David A. Wolfe and Peter G. Jaffe

David A. Wolfe is on the faculty of the Centre for Addiction and Mental Health at the University of Toronto (Canada). Peter G. Jaffe is the founding director and special advisor on violence prevention for the Center for Children and Families in the Justice System, located in London, Ontario, Canada.

Education, particularly of children and teens, is the best way to prevent domestic violence and sexual assault. Educational programs, however, must be carefully designed to reach their target audiences. Programs for children and teens should aim to change social attitudes that encourage domestic violence, such as sexism. Such programs should also teach ways of resolving conflicts without violence and ways to keep safe if violence occurs. Teen programs need to teach teenagers to set clear personal boundaries and develop responsibility. Adult programs should emphasize making people aware of the signs of domestic violence and teaching them what to do if they observe such signs. In the future, the developers of educational programs to prevent domestic violence need to collaborate more with the developers of similar programs aimed at preventing sexual assault. More work also needs to be done to ensure that plans to prevent domestic violence are implemented rather than allowed to languish on an administrator's shelf.

As public recognition of domestic violence (DV) and sexual assault (SA) has reached increasing heights, there has been an outcry for more effective prevention programs. This outcry is based on an understanding of the widespread nature of this problem and the incredible costs to victims and society as a whole. This document summarizes the development of prevention initiatives in these two related areas. However, we caution that DV and SA prevention initiatives and evaluation research on them are in their infancy. Therefore, this review points out trends and promising developments rather than definitive directions in the field. Although the research has many shortcomings it leads to important suggestions for prevention strategies.

Research in this burgeoning field needs to inform prevention. Many of the contributing risk factors for sexual and physical assault perpetration have been identified in childhood and adolescence, and these need to be incorporated into prevention goals. For example, peer attitudes, past experiences of child maltreatment, and substance abuse in adolescence have all been linked to greater risk of dating violence, domestic violence, and sexual assault. Changing the norms and climate about relationships and providing students and teachers with the skills needed to foster healthy relationships is the only viable way to shift from a crisis orientation to one of prevention in response to these related forms of violence.

In preparing this document we took the perspective that DV and SA are gender-linked crimes based in cultural and societal values affecting gender inequality and abuse of power and control. In conjunction with this perspective, DV and SA researchers and practitioners have drawn from a variety of related theoretical perspectives in their prevention efforts, ranging from feminist and sociological views of broad societal influences to individually-focused cognitive and behavioral skill deficits, which are reflected herein.

Prevention Strategies

Prevention efforts are generally considered in terms of primary, secondary, and tertiary. Primary prevention involves efforts to reduce the incidence of a problem among a population before it occurs. The goal of secondary prevention is to target services to select (at-risk) individuals, in an effort to decrease the incidence of a problem by reducing known or suspected risk factors. Tertiary prevention involves attempts to minimize the course of a problem once it is already clearly evident and causing harm, which in the current instance involves the identification of domestic violence and sexual assault perpetrators and victims, control of the behavior and its effect, punishment and/or treatment for the perpetrators, and support for the victims. Because tertiary efforts are intended more as intervention aimed at current needs as well as prevention of future harm, this document reviews only primary and secondary prevention strategies and their current research status.

> *// Providing students and teachers with the skills needed to foster healthy relationships is the only viable way to shift from a crisis orientation to one of prevention [of domestic violence]. //*

In terms of DV and SA, primary prevention strategies introduce new values, thinking processes, and relationship skills to particular population groups that are incompatible with violence and that promote healthy, non-violent relationships. For example, resources can be used to focus on respect, trust, and supportive growth in relationships. A clear advantage is that these efforts can be targeted universally, at broad population groups, such as school-age children or members of a particular community. Secondary prevention efforts are directed toward identified individuals who have exhibited particular behaviors (e.g., dating violence) or possess certain risk factors (e.g., male; prior exposure to violence) that are associated with domestic violence and sexual assault. As described below, examples of sexual assault secondary prevention include programs for first year college students who have a history of victimization or problems with substance abuse, which are associated with dating violence and sexual assault.

Planning Effective Programs

A starting point for prevention programs is deciding on the target age and the best venue for delivering the program. For example, most adolescent programs are designed for a high school (classroom) venue, whereas adult prevention efforts utilize the mass media and workplace to challenge attitudes and behaviors that support violence towards women. There are also considerations regarding variation in program delivery according to the gender of the target audience. Programs on dating violence, for example, may create backlash among boys if they identify the program as an attack on males in general, and unique strategies may be needed for different ages and both sexes. In our experience girls are often more interested in discussing these sensitive issues and willing to role-play social situations relevant to prevention of DV and SA, whereas boys are more resistant and reluctant to do so. Unique strategies for male participation may include involvement of popular male peer and teacher role models, and more graduated approaches to introducing the underlying social issues and factors contributing to DV and SA.

A further consideration in the development of prevention programs in both areas is the identification of the crucial prevention targets. With adolescents and adults, one can explicitly name the problem of domestic violence and sexual assault. However, with younger children prevention efforts are more often tied to the early factors associated with domestic violence and/or sexual assault later in life (e.g., being exposed to domestic violence while growing up).

In general, prevention programs are intended to clarify inappropriate attitudes and behaviors and offer positive alternatives. In essence, most prevention efforts are psychoeducational strategies, rather than treatment services, aimed at a broad sector of the population. Several illustrative programs are described below that reflect the current state of prevention research in domestic violence and sexual assault.

Programs for Children

Schools are an ideal place in which to introduce primary prevention programs to a wide range of children. Much of children's social learning takes place in schools, and influences the development of behaviors and attitudes supportive of interpersonal violence in its many forms. Prevention programs capitalize on these factors by introducing discussion of personal safety and injury prevention in the classroom, and by integrating such discussion within the context of trusting relationships. The material is introduced at a general level of understanding for younger age groups; sexual and physical violence, personal responsibility, and alternatives to violence are more directly approached in high school and college programs.

Community programs have sometimes collaborated with schools in an effort to raise awareness and prevent future violence. One of the key values inherent in these primary prevention programs is the belief that every student needs to be aware of DV and SA. Even if students never become victims or perpetrators, they may have opportunities in the future, as community members, to help others in preventing or stopping these assaults. These model programs sometimes include involvement of parents and other members of the broader community, in an effort to affect broader change.

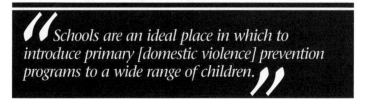

Schools are an ideal place in which to introduce primary [domestic violence] prevention programs to a wide range of children.

One of the first programs to document efforts to prevent domestic violence by working with children in the schools was implemented by the Minnesota Coalition for Battered Women [in 1995], and updated [in 2000] around the themes that "hands are not for hitting" and students' "choice" for alternatives to violence. This excellent program is one of the few that explicitly addresses the root causes of violence, such as racism, classism, sexism, ableism, heterosexism, etc. Preliminary evaluations of this and related programs are promising and indicate that key elements of successful school-based programs include: identifying relationship violence as a form of societal violence; acknowledging that DV and SA are abuse of power and control; creating a high enough level of trust that children can disclose exposure to domestic violence and teachers can make appropriate referrals; teaching safety skills about what to do when domestic violence occurs; and encouraging social skills development like conflict resolution as alternatives to violence.

Programs for Teens

Early- and mid-adolescence offers a unique window of opportunity for prevention efforts to make teens more aware of how violence in relationships can occur and to teach healthy ways of forming intimate relationships. Late adolescence and the early adult years are also critical periods of transition. In fact, college students are seen as so high-risk for partner violence and sexual assault that some researchers argue institutions should provide universal programs to address the magnitude of these issues. When offered opportunities to explore the richness and rewards of relationships, teens and young adults often show a greater interest in learning about choices and responsibilities. Clear messages about personal responsibility and boundaries, delivered in a blame-free manner, are generally acceptable to this age group, whereas lectures and warnings are less helpful.

> *Early- and mid-adolescence offers a unique window of opportunity for prevention efforts.*

DV and SA prevention among this critical age group has focused on dating violence that often includes, by definition, psychological, physical, and sexual abuse. Although the literature approaches dating violence and sexual assault prevention as separate topics, they overlap considerably, especially from a prevention standpoint. Programs on rape prevention focus on violence committed by strangers, acquaintances, work colleagues, and intimate partners, which overlap with dating violence initiatives in terms of lessons about inappropriate attitudes and behaviors. More recently programs have incorporated content on the influence of drugs and alcohol and, in particular, "date-rape" drugs that allow perpetrators to incapacitate potential victims. Recognizing the overlap between DV and SA is important, without allowing drugs and alcohol to become an excuse for the perpetrator or an opportunity to blame the victim.

Primary prevention programs delivered universally through high schools often involve activities aimed at increasing awareness and dispelling myths about relationship violence and sexual assault. Such activities include school auditorium presentations involving videotapes, plays, professional theatre groups, or a speech from a DV or SA survivor; classroom discussions facilitated by teachers or service providers; programs and curricula that encourage students to examine attitudes and behaviors that promote or tolerate violence; or peer support groups. Some school-based programs have resulted in youth-initiated prevention activities such as theatrical presentations to younger children and marches and other social protests against violence.

A [2001] controlled evaluation of universal sexual assault prevention involved a coeducational program for teens on preventing sexual coercion in dating situations. The program involved challenging existing attitudes about coercive sexual behavior, and learning ways to deal with unwanted sexual advances through clear communication. The program was innovative in its use of video and an interactive "virtual date." Results indicate that students with more negative attitudes about sexual assault benefited the most from the program, which supports the use of educational strategies to reduce risk factors among this age group. Similar initiatives have been undertaken with college-aged populations.

Although DV and SA cross all races and social classes, some sexual assault prevention programs are aimed at high-risk groups, such as males from abusive family backgrounds, in an attempt to reduce sexual assault by targeting rape myths and coercive behaviors. For example, P.A. Schewe and W. O' Donohue evaluated cognitive-behavioral approaches that address beliefs that promote or condone coercive sexual behavior, as well as increasing empathy for the plight of sexual assault victims. A strength of this study was its involvement of participants from diverse cultural backgrounds, which were randomly assigned to treatment or control conditions. Using self-report, this investigation determined that cognitive-behavioral intervention was effective primarily at changing rape-supporting attitudes and beliefs in a high-risk sample. Other researchers have approached high-risk groups, such as fraternities, which may support inappropriate male attitudes that condone sexual assault. A promising approach in this regard involves young men's groups that engender empathy for sexual assault survivors, which found a significant reduction in rape myth acceptance over a seven-month period.

Changing Attitudes

Recent school-based dating violence prevention programs have also shown favorable outcomes in terms of reducing reports of physical, sexual, and emotional abuse towards and by dating partners. Primary prevention programs have approached this topic through school-based curricula that address specific skills and knowledge opposing abusive behavior toward romantic partners. These curricula have primarily used didactic approaches to orient students to the different ways in which abuse and violence may be expressed, and examining their own attitudes and gender role stereotypes. V.A. Foshee et al., for example, examined the effects of a dating violence prevention program ("Safe Dates") on psychological, physical, and sexual abuse in young adolescents. Over 1500 grade 8 and 9 students participated in 10 classroom sessions and related activities, such as a poster contest. This is one of the few studies that included a follow-up to explore long-term prevention effects. Although some of the positive behavioral changes had disappeared at a one-year follow-up, some of the critical changes in variables that mediate dating violence (e.g., dating violence norms, conflict management skills, and awareness of community services for dating violence) were maintained.

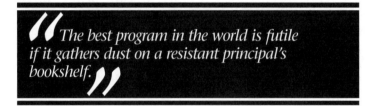

The best program in the world is futile if it gathers dust on a resistant principal's bookshelf.

In addition to school-based programs for adolescents, community-based programs with secondary prevention goals have been developed to target youth at-risk of dating violence. The Youth Relationships Project was developed to assist adults in empowering youth to end violence in relationships (their own and that of their peers) through education, skill development, and social competence. The program material takes teens from high-risk (i.e., abusive) backgrounds through a process of learning about the issue, about themselves, and then expands their efforts to affect change within their peer groups, the teen culture and the broader community. It reflects an incremental strategy aimed at self-awareness and social change (i.e., examining oneself first, and moving on to one's peers, school environment, social institutions, and cultural influences), which is delivered through an 18-session program in community settings. Two-year follow-up results involving random assignment to the intervention or control condition support this approach in reducing threatening behavior toward dating partners, as well as physical and emotional abuse perpetration.

Public awareness campaigns such as public service announcements and advertisements are common approaches to primary prevention of DV and SA with adults. These campaigns typically provide information regarding the warning signs of violence and community resources for victims and perpetrators. [In the last quarter of the twentieth century] sexual assault centers and shelters for abused women have played a leadership role in these public awareness strategies. A comprehensive public education campaign developed by the Family Violence Prevention Fund (FVPF) in collaboration with the Advertising Council included television advertisements delivering the message that there is no excuse for domestic violence and making referrals to local domestic violence services. Telephone surveys conducted over two years showed decreases in the number of people who said they did not know what to do about domestic violence, did not believe it was necessary to report it, felt it was no one else's business, and believed that the problem of domestic violence was exaggerated by the media. However, the results also showed that men were more likely than women to believe women provoke men into physically abusing them, and to feel that the media exaggerated the prevalence and harms of domestic violence. . . .

Broader Prevention Efforts

We are currently at a crossroads regarding the role of school- and community-based programming in preventing domestic violence and sexual assault. There has never been greater awareness of the issue of violence, but at the same time society has never been more polarized in deciding how to respond: reactively or proactively. There is a clear need for these two fields to become more integrated in their approach to prevention. Historically, there have been separate movements to address sexual assault and domestic violence, which have led to different services such as rape crisis centers and shelters for battered women. Underlying these social problems are similar risk factors at the individual, family, community, and societal levels. Recognizing these similarities should lead to a common purpose in prevention efforts and greater collaboration among local, state, and federal government initiatives, social agencies, and community mobilization efforts. It is now necessary to move beyond small local programs scattered across various communities to comprehensive evaluations and research that will support broader prevention efforts.

As the field of DV and SA prevention develops, there will be a remaining challenge to ensure programs are implemented on a comprehensive and consistent basis. The best program in the world is futile if it gathers dust on a resistant principal's bookshelf, surrounded by the silence of other educators, parents, and students. An open, collaborative process based on respect, trust, flexibility, and communication is needed to advance evaluation efforts with community- and school-based programs. Despite significant challenges, prevention efforts remain a very promising approach to reducing domestic violence and sexual assault.

11

Health Care Professionals Need to Help Prevent Domestic Violence

Esta Soler

Esta Soler is president of the Family Violence Prevention Fund, a nonprofit organization working to end domestic violence and help families whose lives are devastated by abuse.

Domestic violence is a major cause of physical and mental health problems in women and children. These problems are likely to bring abused women and children to the attention of health care professionals. Health care providers therefore can play a vital role in detecting family violence and preventing further damage. Doctors and other health care workers should screen their patients routinely for domestic violence, just as they now screen for conditions such as diabetes, cancer, and HIV/AIDS. In fifteen states, this kind of screening has been successfully used to identify and help victims of domestic violence. However, legislation is needed to provide more funding, research, and training that will enable health care professionals to detect and prevent domestic violence.

D omestic violence is a health care problem of epidemic proportions. Experts estimate that 25 to 31 percent of women in the United States have been abused by an intimate partner at some point in their lives. In addition to the immediate trauma

Esta Soler, testimony before the U.S. Senate Subcommittee on Public Health, Committee on Health, Education, Labor, and Pensions, Washington, DC, April 25, 2002.

and injury caused by abuse, domestic violence can cause serious physical and mental health problems that last a lifetime. It contributes to chronic conditions including neck, back and pelvic pain, ulcers, migraines and arthritis, and victims of domestic violence suffer from higher rates of mental health problems including depression, anxiety, posttraumatic stress disorder and suicide attempts. Patients experiencing abuse also are more likely to have adverse health risk behaviors such as smoking, substance/alcohol abuse and poor diet.

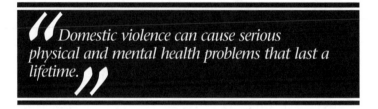

Domestic violence can cause serious physical and mental health problems that last a lifetime.

Battered women can have great difficulty accessing health care. The control exercised by batterers—and the isolation that results—often mean that battered women are less likely to engage in preventative health behaviors and to make or keep well woman/well child appointments, have mammograms and access early pre-natal care. Managing chronic illnesses such as asthma, diabetes and hypertension may also be problematic for abused women because batterers frequently deny them access to money and transportation and prevent them from keeping medical appointments or getting medicine.

In particular, pregnant women are at a risk. Some 240,000 pregnant women each year are abused by their partners. A recent study showed that homicide, including intimate partner homicide, is the leading cause of death for pregnant women. Abused pregnant women are also significantly more likely to experience complications of pregnancy including low weight gain, anemia, infections and first- and second-trimester bleeding. Victims of domestic violence are more likely to have gynecological problems during pregnancy than women who are not abused. In addition, battered women have higher rates of sexually transmitted infections including HIV, as well as depression, suicide attempts, and tobacco, alcohol and illicit drug use.

Children can also suffer greatly when they are exposed to domestic violence. Three to ten million children witness domestic violence each year in the United States. The greatest immediate risk for children who live in violent homes is that they will be physically abused. In 30 to 60 percent of families experiencing intimate partner violence, children also are abused. Children who are exposed to violence are more likely to become both perpetrators and victims of domestic violence. They often show symptoms associated with posttraumatic stress disorder and they are more likely to have cognitive and behavioral problems including depression, anxiety and violence towards peers. They are more likely to attempt suicide, abuse drugs and alcohol, run away from home, engage in teenage prostitution and commit sexual assault. Fortunately, children can often overcome the harm caused by witnessing abuse with interventions and developmentally appropriate mental health services. However, without these interventions, the impact of childhood exposure to violence often lasts a lifetime. Adults who experienced adverse childhood experiences, including domestic violence, are more likely than other adults to smoke, abuse drugs or alcohol, and suffer from depression and obesity. They are also at significantly higher risk for health problems associated with those poor health behaviors, including cardiopulmonary disease, heart disease, diabetes and suicide attempts.

The Urgent Need for Screening

The health care system often plays an important role in identifying and preventing serious public health problems, and we believe the health care system can play a unique and pivotal role in domestic violence prevention and intervention. Virtually every American woman interacts with the health care system at some point in her life—whether it is for routine care, pregnancy, childbirth, illness, injury or to seek care for her child. Women who are abused also frequently seek health care for illnesses and injuries resulting from the violence they face. In fact, a November 1998 report of the National Institute of Justice and the Centers for Disease Control and Prevention found that women make 693,933 visits to health care providers per year as a result of injuries resulting from physical assault. The majority of these visits are for treatment of injuries that were inflicted by intimate partners. This study only measured the impact of specific injuries directly related to physical assault; experts believe the numbers would be significantly higher if it had examined visits for other health problems related to domestic violence and how abuse affects the management of other illnesses.

We are convinced that the models developed to prevent other chronic health problems can be effectively applied to domestic violence. Recent experience with AIDS, smoking, breast cancer and cardiovascular disease support the efficacy of screening as a tool to identify health problems and intervene effectively. Domestic violence is more prevalent than diabetes and breast and cervical cancer—conditions that health care professionals screen for on a routine basis—yet screening for domestic violence is much more rare.

By not screening for domestic violence and inquiring about abuse, health care providers often fail to recognize or address the underlying cause of battered women's health problems. Even when domestic violence results in injuries that were clearly inflicted by another person, health care providers too often treat and record the injuries without inquiring about the cause.

Providers also miss opportunities to intervene early, before a woman is injured, by not routinely screening for violence. A study published in the *Journal of the American Medical Association* in August 1999 found that less than ten percent of primary care physicians routinely screen for domestic violence during regular office visits. These wasted opportunities literally cost battered women their lives.

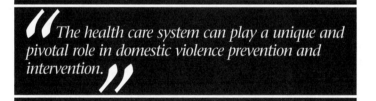

The health care system can play a unique and pivotal role in domestic violence prevention and intervention.

Fortunately, practice is beginning to change. For almost two decades, a host of national health care organizations and experts have called for programs that educate health care providers about intimate partner violence and promote routine screening and intervention. The American Medical Association, American Nurses Association, American Psychological Association, American College of Obstetricians and Gynecologists, American Academy of Pediatrics and, most recently, the Institute of Medicine have all developed guidelines or recommendations for improving providers' response to family violence. In addition, the Family Violence Prevention Fund's "national screening for intimate partner violence consensus guidelines" are widely used.

Catching Abuse Early

Routine screening, with its focus on early identification and its capacity to reach patients whether or not symptoms are immediately apparent, is the starting point to improve medical practice for domestic violence. Routine and multiple face-to-face screenings by skilled health care providers can markedly increase the identification of domestic violence. Routine—rather than indicator-based—screening increases opportunities to identify and intervene with patients who present with symptoms not generally associated with domestic violence. Several studies demonstrate the importance of conducting inquiries in private settings and using straightforward, nonjudgmental questions, preferably asked verbally by a health care practitioner.

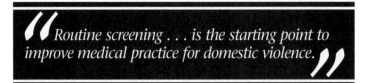

Routine screening . . . is the starting point to improve medical practice for domestic violence.

This kind of screening gives women a valuable opportunity to tell their providers about their experiences with abuse, and battered women report that one of the most important parts of their interactions with their physicians is being listened to about their abuse. When victims of domestic violence or those at risk for abuse are identified early, providers can help them understand their options, live more safely within the relationship or safely leave the relationship. In one study, a ten-minute intervention was proven highly effective in increasing the safety of women abused during pregnancy. All these interventions can lead to reduced morbidity and mortality.

This work is being successfully tested. The Family Violence Prevention Fund is working in 15 states to improve the health care response to domestic violence. These state-based programs are demonstrating that improved collaboration and coordination between battered women's advocates, health care leaders, policy makers and public health officials can strengthen health care services to victims of domestic violence.

Due in part to these efforts, screening and intervention is becoming the standard of care. More than 20 states now have laws addressing the health care system's response to domestic violence. The Joint Commission on the Accreditation of Health Care Organizations developed standards for emergency departments about how to respond to abuse, and has now expanded those guidelines for all departments in hospitals. The coding clinic guidelines issued by the American Medical Association, the American Hospital Association and the American Health Information Management Association also require coding domestic violence in medical records.

Finally, research shows that patients support screening practices. In fact, in four different studies of survivors of abuse, 70 to 81 percent of the patients asked said that they would like their health care providers to ask them privately about intimate partner violence.

Legislative Support for Screening

Because domestic violence is so prevalent and has such detrimental health, social and economic consequences, there is an urgent need for more serious and ongoing attention from the health care system and from our elected officials.

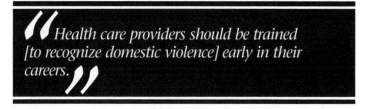

Health care providers should be trained [to recognize domestic violence] early in their careers.

We are heartened, however, by the actions of this committee [the Subcommittee on Public Health of the Senate Committee on Health, Education, Labor, and Pensions] and efforts of many Senators . . . on behalf of battered women and their children. Senator [Paul] Wellstone's Screening and Services Act will make a tremendous difference to abused women and their children. By funding demonstration projects to improve collaboration between the health care system and advocates for victims of abuse, this legislation will help ensure that women are treated appropriately and that a full system of care and services will be available to them. This bill will lead to more effective interventions, more coordinated systems of care, greater resources to educate health care providers and, ultimately, more women disclosing abuse and receiving help. In addition, providers who can recognize abuse in their patients will more effectively address the health implications of the violence their patients are experiencing. Without resources to promote this collaboration, efforts may be duplicative and health systems will struggle with the grave consequences of their failure to effectively help patients experiencing domestic violence for years to come.

> *Children who witness domestic violence are more likely [than other children] to exhibit behavioral and physical health problems.*

The legislation also targets specific funds to federally qualified health centers and requires providers participating in the National Health Service Corps to be trained in the dynamics of domestic violence. Local community health centers deal with family violence every day, and many are doing an excellent job of identifying, treating and referring patients, when appropriate. However, much more work needs to be done to ensure that providers throughout the nation have the knowledge and specific training necessary to intervene appropriately.

Training Health Care Providers

Other legislative proposals being addressed during this hearing are critical to a strengthened health care response to domestic violence. Health care providers should be trained early in their professional careers. Medical and nursing schools, as well as dental and physician assistant programs, need to teach their students in a substantive way about domestic violence. Providers often report that they don't view domestic violence as a health issue, but rather as a social problem, and one that they're not equipped to handle in our current health care environment. If we train physicians and other providers early about the health care implications of domestic violence, we will have greater success in making preventive screening routine.

Senator [Barbara] Boxer's bill, S. 518, The Domestic Violence Identification and Referral Act, will encourage schools that train health professionals to give their students the education necessary to properly screen for, identify and treat victims of domestic violence. Its approach of providing preference in federal funding to programs that do provide "significant training" also will have no budget implications, since it will only address the awarding of grants that have already been funded.

Funding for Research

In addition, we need funding to improve the research around family violence and the quality of the training for health care providers and researchers. Senators [Richard] Durbin and [Susan] Collins are sponsoring S. 2009, the Family Violence Prevention Act, to provide much needed funding for research. Based on a recent report from the Institute of Medicine, this legislation will support research in medical education and effective interventions to address family violence. Specifically, we applaud the bill's focus on outcomes-based research and effective interventions as they relate to women's safety and the impact of witnessing violence on children. Their bill targets areas where new research needs to be focused, including:

- Patterns of health care utilization by victims of family violence, the effects that family violence has on victims' health status, and the health care costs attributable to family violence;
- The effects of family violence on other health conditions and preventive health behaviors;
- The relationship between childhood exposure to domestic violence and child and adult health and safety;
- Effective interventions for children exposed to violence;
- Strategies to inform and mobilize public action for prevention; and
- The effects of mandatory reporting requirements on victims' safety and likelihood of receiving appropriate care and services.

We are particularly appreciative of their efforts to include domestic violence experts as members of a team that will review the types of research funded, further building the bridge between the research and advocacy communities.

Mental Health Services

Finally, we see great hope in the two bills introduced by Senator [John] Edwards to improve mental health services for victims of domestic violence. While not all battered women experience mental health or substance abuse problems, many women and their children do need and request services to deal with the effects of the violence. The consequences of not receiving help can be severe. Twenty-nine percent of all women who attempt suicide are battered, 37 percent of battered women have symptoms of depression, 46 percent have symptoms of anxiety disorder, and 45 percent experience post-traumatic stress disorder. Children who witness domestic violence are more likely to exhibit behavioral and physical health problems including depression, anxiety and violence towards peers. As noted earlier, they are also more likely to engage in a host of harmful behaviors.

Unfortunately, many of the women who need mental health services for themselves or their families often lack the resources to access services in their communities or live in communities where services simply are not available. The Counseling in Shelters Act and the Women in Trauma Act would give women and their children access to needed mental health services in a safe and caring setting. Importantly, they would also improve coordination between and support cross-training for domestic violence advocates and mental health providers. This legislation would fill a critical void in our efforts to help battered women and their children repair their lives.

12

Counseling for Couples Does Not Prevent Domestic Violence

Phyllis B. Frank and Gail Kadison Golden

Phyllis B. Frank is director of the Community Change Project at the Volunteer Counseling Service of Rockland County, Inc., in the state of New York. Gail Kadison Golden is a social worker and clinical director of Volunteer Counseling Services in Rockland County, New York.

Couple counseling is often useful for easing the problems of troubled marriages, but it is not appropriate for marriages marred by domestic violence. Women who are being abused by their partners are unlikely to feel free to speak openly to their counselors when their abuser is present. Furthermore, women who do tell the truth about the abuse may be at serious risk when they return home with their violent partners. Therapists should therefore arrange to counsel women separately from their abusive partners. Couple counseling should only be used in violent marriages after the batterer has ended the abuse and both partners have separately requested this kind of help.

Therapists and counselors in a variety of settings are frequently called on to counsel couples who seek help with aspects of their lives that range from assistance with child rearing to communication, sexuality, and other relationship issues. It is only in recent years, however, that we have begun to recognize

93

that many couples who seek marriage and family counseling do so against a background of domestic violence.

Current estimates suggest that in 50 percent of all marriages there will be at least one physically abusive episode during the course of the marriage. This estimate does not include the untold numbers of women who are systematically abused through nonphysical patterns of coercive and controlling tactics inflicted on them by their partners. The result of this emotional and psychological abuse, often reported by victims to be equally or even more damaging than physical violence, is women who are not free—to speak, to do, or to be.

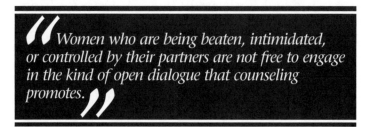

Women who are being beaten, intimidated, or controlled by their partners are not free to engage in the kind of open dialogue that counseling promotes.

This reality raises important issues for therapists and counselors. We know that both partners, for very different reasons, are generally reluctant to disclose information about his abuse and violence in their relationship. To balance this fact, we must raise our own consciousness about all forms of men's abuse of women in heterosexual couple relationships and assume responsibility for learning about the climate of control that he has created when the couple is not in our office. To accomplish this, it is imperative to interview each partner alone and to ask specific questions related to violence and other controlling strategies. Failure to gather this information can result in counseling that at best is a waste of time and at worst colludes with and perpetuates men's violence, thus further endangering women.

Therapy Can Endanger Women

Women who are being beaten, intimidated, or controlled by their partner are not free to engage in the kind of open dialogue that counseling promotes. In fact, a woman who does speak openly to a therapist or counselor in the presence of an abusive partner may be in serious danger from him when she returns home.

Those who counsel couples whose relationships are marked

by stated or unacknowledged violence are conducting sessions in the presence of a powerful censor. Men who abuse their partners control their relationships by instituting serious restrictions and rules. The women know what those rules are, although often they cannot articulate them. The therapist who knows nothing of these rules may unwittingly encourage a woman to cross a line that will seriously endanger her.

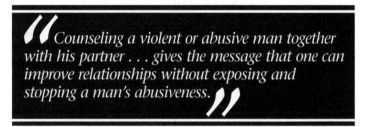

Counseling a violent or abusive man together with his partner . . . gives the message that one can improve relationships without exposing and stopping a man's abusiveness.

Therapists or counselors who are aware of abuse in a relationship and who agree to see the couple together collude in another way with a set of damaging insinuations that further imperil women. Although the very act of working with a couple in which there is an abusive partner implies that the problem is in the relationship, it is not. Abusive men are solely responsible for their abusive behavior. Conversely, the victim of abusive behavior has no part in the attacks against her. No matter how provocative or inappropriate women's behavior, it neither justifies nor excuses men's abuse.

When working with violent relationships therapists have been tempted to encourage women to learn to alter their behaviors so as not to provoke their partner's abuse. However, women cannot. Because her behavior is in no way responsible for her partner's abusiveness, any changes she makes will not be the deciding factor in his stopping the abuse.

Centuries of Male Domination

Men are abusive to their women partners because of thousands of years of patriarchal culture, institutions, and laws that have permitted, condoned, and even encouraged these actions. Counseling a violent or abusive man together with his partner conceals and therefore perpetuates such sanctions. It also gives the message that one can improve relationships without exposing and stopping a man's abusiveness. In fact, the man must end his abusiveness (and his sense of entitlement to his partner and her services) before couple work can be even considered.

It is enormously helpful if therapists and counselors providing treatment understand the cultural context of domestic violence and the implicit permission for men to abuse that continues to be embedded in our institutions and in our communities. With this framework, strong, confrontive, educational counseling that separates men from their partners, defines the spectrum of abuse, and holds abusers solely accountable for their actions, has the possibility of supporting men to stop their abusive mistreatment. Such intervention is the best protection for a woman from the therapeutic abuse perpetrated by assuming that she has a part in provoking her partner's behavior.

Arresting men who batter is an effective "therapeutic" intervention *when* there is a coordinated criminal justice response and the crime is taken seriously by the courts. Therapy will have a much greater chance of being useful in a community where there is a public commitment to end domestic violence. Conversely, family systems therapy, which isolates the problem in the relationship, endangers battered women. So does mediation, which assumes that the two parties have equal standing in a dispute and the ability to negotiate fairly. In fact, "mediation of an assault" is a conflict in terms. The power imbalance and the violence preclude equitable negotiations between the two parties.

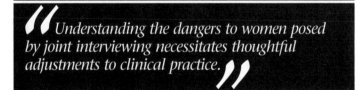

Understanding the dangers to women posed by joint interviewing necessitates thoughtful adjustments to clinical practice.

What social workers do not know about domestic violence can kill their clients. Social workers have been trained in a variety of approaches (for example, behavior modification, family systems, and psychoanalysis) that seem generally useful with other kinds of clients and issues. Imposing these models on work with men who are abusive and their partners, however, not only may prove ineffective but also may actually exacerbate the danger of his assault. The past decades of groundbreaking work in the field of domestic abuse have yielded clear, usable information. It is incumbent on us to be open to theory and analysis that come out of the work that has been done with thousands of abused women. Therapists and counselors in hospitals, courts, schools, mental health clinics, and the like are in a unique position to confront the issue of abuse by asking the right questions and by disallowing treatment interventions that perpetuate the problem.

How to Help Women

Understanding the dangers to women posed by joint interviewing necessitates thoughtful adjustments to clinical practice. Because mental health workers cannot know what truly happens behind closed doors, and because statistically such large numbers of women are not safe, ethical practice requires that we craft all of our interventions with the understanding that we may inadvertently place women at risk of harm from her partner. The intake is especially important since it is the first contact taking place in the absence of much important information. One family service agency, after years of trial and error, has found the following procedures to be very helpful:

When a person calls to request couple counseling they will be given an appointment. There is no attempt to telephone screen any caller regarding the possibility that a woman is experiencing abuse from her partner. In all instances, we feel it is in the best interest of women to meet with an intake worker, even if she later declines treatment recommendations that may not include couple counseling. We advise callers that couple intakes require about two hours and, as a routine part of the assessment, both parties will be seen separately before being seen together. It is important to leave enough time. Two hours seems about right.

Women are always seen first. A thorough interview is done to determine, as best as possible, whether a partner is perpetrating physical, emotional, sexual or financial abuse against her. If it is determined that this is indeed the case, information is given about domestic abuse, including local domestic violence service agencies and the reason why separate, individual counseling will be offered. We review with her that after we see him, we will meet with them as a couple, very briefly, to give our suggestions for treatment. We will share with her as to what we plan to tell them when meeting together.

Battered women's advocates suggest that in order to assure her safety, we should not focus on his abusive behavior as the reason for treatment decisions. They suggest that we say something like:

"At this time, the level of marital conflict is too intense for couple counseling. Therefore we will start with individual sessions, and then review." Or: "At this time, each party has individual issues that need to be worked on before couple counseling would help." We can use the inference that couple counseling may be arranged at some time in the future.

Women should be told in advance what we will say and her input should be sought. She knows him best and may have some further thought about how to present things to him. After he is seen, the couple should be seen together for a very short time, simply to present our recommendations.

Even if either partner or both partners decline treatment, women will have been given valuable information about domestic abuse and resources available to help her now or at some time in the future.

Organizations to Contact

Battered Women's Justice Project (BWJP)
(800) 903-0111
Web site: www.bwjp.org

The Battered Women's Justice Project is a collaborative effort of three organizations that have pioneered innovative civil and criminal justice responses to domestic violence: the Pennsylvania Coalition Against Domestic Violence, the National Clearinghouse for the Defense of Battered Women, and Minnesota Program Development, Inc. The Pennsylvania group coordinates the BWJP Civil Justice Office, the National Clearinghouse operates the BWJP Defense Office, and the Minnesota group, also known as the Duluth Domestic Abuse Intervention Project, manages the BWJP Criminal Justice Office. The BWJP undertakes state, local, and national projects to make community organizations and governmental agencies involved in the civil and criminal justice response to domestic violence more accountable for ensuring the safety of battered women and their families. Its Web site includes access to articles and links.

FaithTrust Institute
2400 N. Forty-fifth St., #10, Seattle, WA 98103
(206) 634-1903
Web site: www.faithtrustinstitute.org

Founded in 1977 by the Reverend Marie M. Fortune and headquartered in Seattle, Washington, the FaithTrust Institute is an interreligious educational resource aiming to engage religious leaders in the task of ending sexual and domestic abuse and to be a bridge between religious and secular communities. It was formerly called the Center for Prevention of Sexual and Domestic Violence. It publishes a newsletter, *Working Together*, and a journal, the *Journal of Religion and Abuse*, as well as an electronic newsletter.

Family Violence Prevention Fund
383 Rhode Island St., Suite 304, San Francisco, CA 94103-5133
(415) 252-8900
e-mail: info@endabuse.org • Web site: http://endabuse.org

The Family Violence Prevention Fund works to prevent violence within the home and in the community and to help those whose lives have been devastated by violence. It educates men and youth, promotes involvement of communities and community leaders in efforts to end family violence, and attempts to transform the way health care providers, police, judges, employers, and others address violence. Its Web site includes news, resources, and descriptions of programs focusing on children, health, immigrant women, public policy, and the workplace.

Legal Momentum
395 Hudson St., New York, NY 10014
(212) 925-6635
Web site: www.legalmomentum.org

Formerly the National Organization of Women (NOW) Legal Education and Defense Fund, Legal Momentum uses the power of law and innovative public policy to advance the rights of women and girls. It is a national legal advocate for these rights, focusing on economic justice, freedom from gender-based violence, and equality under the law. Its Web site includes news, legal updates, and publications concerning violence against women.

Men Stopping Violence, Inc.
533 W. Howard Ave., Decatur, GA 30030
(404) 270-9894
e-mail: msv@menstoppingviolence.org
Web site: www.menstoppingviolence.org/index.php

Men Stopping Violence is a social change organization working locally, nationally, and internationally to dismantle belief systems, social structures, and institutional practices that oppress women and children and dehumanize men. The group's efforts to end men's violence against women are part of a larger attempt to end all forms of oppression, including those based on race, class, age, and sexual orientation as well as gender. The Men Stopping Violence Web site includes news, fact sheets, and descriptions of the group's programs.

Ms. Foundation for Women
120 Wall St., 33rd Fl., New York, NY 10005
(212) 742-2300
e-mail: info@ms.foundation.org • Web site: www.ms.foundation.org

The Ms. Foundation provides leadership, expertise, and financial support to bring about changes in public consciousness, law, philanthropy, and public policy that will promote a more equitable society. It sponsors Take Our Daughters and Sons to Work Day. Its Web site includes news, a newsletter, annual reports, and publications such as *Safety and Justice for All* (examining the relationship between the women's antiviolence movement and the criminal legal system) and *Beyond Surviving* (proposal for a movement to prevent child sexual abuse).

National Center on Domestic and Sexual Violence
7800 Shoal Creek Blvd., Suite 120-N, Austin, TX 78757
(512) 407-9020
Web site: www.ncdsv.org

The National Center on Domestic and Sexual Violence trains professionals who work with victims and perpetrators of these crimes, including professionals in law enforcement and criminal justice, health care, counseling and social work, and advocacy and service provision. It also works with local, state, and federal agencies; state and national organizations; educators, researchers, community religious leaders, media, policy makers, the military, and others to reduce domestic and sexual violence. The publications section of its Web site provides links to a wide variety of articles on topics related to domestic violence, such as dating violence, immigration, mental health, and protection orders. These resources include newspaper articles, academic reports, organization position papers, and much more.

National Coalition Against Domestic Violence
PO Box 18749, Denver, CO 80218
(303) 839-1852
Web site: www.ncadv.org

The National Coalition Against Domestic Violence, founded in 1978, believes that the roots of violence against women and children lie in societal inequities and abuses of power, and it works to change these inequities. It builds coalitions at the local, state, regional, and national levels; supports community-based programs for battered women and children; and encourages public education, policy development, and innovative legislation. Its Web site includes statistics, research, links, reading and video lists, and suggestions for public advocacy.

National Council on Child Abuse and Family Violence
1025 Connecticut Ave. NW, Washington, DC 20036
(202) 429-6695
Web site: www.nccafv.org

The National Council on Child Abuse and Family Violence has provided violence prevention services for children and families in all fifty states, Puerto Rico, and the U.S. Virgin Islands since 1984. It works especially to prevent family violence between generations, including child abuse and elder abuse as well as spouse/partner abuse. It provides public awareness and education materials, consultation on program and resource development, and technical assistance and training in the United States and internationally. Its Web site includes articles about child and family abuse, information about programs, fact sheets about different types of abuse, and other resources.

National Network to End Domestic Violence (NNEDV)
660 Pennsylvania Ave. SE, Suite 303, Washington, DC 20003
(202) 543-5566
Web site: www.nnedv.org

The NNEDV is a social change organization representing state domestic violence coalitions. It is dedicated to creating a social, political, and economic environment in which violence against women no longer exists. Its focus is legal and legislative action, such as encouraging legislators to renew the Violence Against Women Act. The organization's Web site describes its programs and provides news and links to related sites.

National Resource Center on Domestic Violence
6400 Flank Dr., Suite 1300, Harrisburg, PA 17112
(800) 537-2238
Web site: www.nrcdv.org

The National Resource Center on Domestic Violence (NRCDV) is a project of the Pennsylvania Coalition Against Domestic Violence, funded by a grant from the U.S. Department of Health and Human Services.

Founded in 1993, it is a component of a national network of domestic violence resources. It provides support, technical assistance, training, and information to all organizations and individuals working to end violence in the lives of victims and their children. Its Web site includes a video list and a catalog of its research library. This group also sponsors the National Electronic Network on Violence Against Women, or VAWnet, which has a separate Web site at www.vawnet.org. VAWnet provides a substantial number of articles describing research on domestic violence, mostly for an academic or professional audience. Its "In the News" section offers hundreds of links to articles and audio and video resources on domestic and sexual violence and related issues.

National Sexual Violence Resource Center
123 N. Enola Dr., Enola, PA 17025
(877) 739-3895
e-mail: ohcinfo@cdc.gov • Web site: www.nsvrc.org

Funded by a grant from the Division of Violence Prevention, part of the Centers for Disease Control and Prevention (CDC), the National Sexual Violence Resource Center is a project of the Pennsylvania Coalition Against Rape. It acts as a national information and resource hub relating to all aspects of sexual violence. Activities include collecting, reviewing, cataloging, and disseminating information about sexual violence; coordinating efforts with other organizations; providing technical assistance; and maintaining a Web site. The Web site features links to sexual assault resources and information about research and upcoming events. It also publishes a newsletter twice a year.

National Violence Against Women Prevention Research Center
(843) 792-2945
Web site: www.vawprevention.org

The National Violence Against Women Prevention Research Center advances prevention research and fosters collaboration among practitioners, policy makers, advocates, and researchers working to prevent violence against women. It is funded by a grant from the Centers for Disease Control and Prevention. Its Web site includes academic articles and information about federal and state legal policy and judicial action, program evaluation, and recent news.

Office on Violence Against Women
800 K St. NW, Suite 920, Washington, DC 20530
(202) 307-6026
Web site: www.ojp.usdoj.gov/vawo

The Office on Violence Against Women is overseen by the Office of Justice Programs, part of the U.S. Department of Justice (DOJ). It handles the DOJ's legal and policy issues regarding violence against women and helps to implement the mandates of the Violence Against Women Act and related legislation. It awards grants to help state, local, and tribal governments and community agencies train personnel, help victims of domestic violence, and prosecute perpetrators of violence. Its Web site includes a number of resources related to legal aspects of domestic violence, such as research papers and a survey of federal and state laws.

Bibliography

Books

Lundy Bancroft — *When Dad Hurts Mom: Helping Your Children Heal the Wounds of Witnessing Abuse.* New York: Putnam, 2004.

Lundy Bancroft — *Why Does He Do That? Inside the Minds of Angry and Controlling Men.* New York: Putnam, 2002.

Dawn Bradley Berry — *The Domestic Violence Sourcebook.* 3rd ed. Los Angeles: Lowell House, 2000.

Susan Brewster — *To Be an Anchor in the Storm: A Guide for Family and Friends of Abused Women.* 2nd ed. Emeryville, CA: Seal Press/Avalon, 2000.

Christina Dalpiaz — *Breaking Free, Starting Over: Parenting in the Aftermath of Family Violence.* New York: Praeger, 2004.

Meg Kennedy Dugan and Roger R. Hock — *It's My Life Now: Starting Over After an Abusive Relationship or Domestic Violence.* New York: Routledge, 2000.

Kevin A. Fall, Shareen Howard, and June A. Ford — *Alternatives to Domestic Violence: A Homework Manual for Battering Intervention Groups.* New York: Brunner-Routledge, 2004.

Connie May Fowler — *When Katie Wakes: A Memoir.* New York: Ballantine, 2003.

Patricia Riddle Gaddis — *Dangerous Dating: Helping Young Women Break Out of Abusive Relationships.* New York: Random/Waterbrook, 2000.

David M. Haugen, ed. — *Opposing Viewpoints: Domestic Violence.* San Diego: Greenhaven, 2005.

Neil S. Jacobson and John M. Gottman — *When Men Batter Women: New Insights into Ending Abusive Relationships.* New York: Simon & Schuster, 1998.

Thomas B. James — *Domestic Violence: 12 Things You Aren't Supposed to Know.* San Diego: Aventine, 2003.

Pamela Jayne — *Ditch That Jerk: Dealing with Men Who Control and Hurt Women.* Alameda, CA: Hunter House, 2000.

Beth Leventhal and Sandra E. Lundy, eds. — *Same-Sex Domestic Violence: Strategies for Change.* Thousand Oaks, CA: Sage, 1999.

David J. Livingston — *Healing Violent Men: A Model for Christian Communities.* Minneapolis, MN: Fortress, 2002.

Donileen R. Loseke, Richard J. Gelles, and Mary M. Cavenaugh, eds.	*Current Controversies on Family Violence.* 2nd ed. Thousand Oaks, CA: Sage, 2004.
Al Miles	*Ending Violence in Teen Dating Relationships: A Resource Guide for Parents and Pastors.* Minneapolis, MN: Augsburg, 2005.
Linda G. Mills	*Insult to Injury: Rethinking Our Responses to Intimate Abuse.* Princeton, NJ: Princeton University Press, 2003.
Noelle Nelson	*Dangerous Relationships: How to Identify and Respond to the Seven Warning Signs of a Troubled Relationship.* Cambridge, MA: Perseus, 2001.
Michael Paymar	*Violent No More: Helping Men End Domestic Abuse.* 2nd ed. Alameda, CA: Hunter House, 1999.
Steven S. Richmond	*Terms of Enforcement: Making Men Pay for What They've Done.* Victoria, BC: Trafford, 2002.
Albert R. Roberts, ed.	*Handbook of Domestic Violence Intervention Strategies: Policies, Programs, and Legal Remedies.* New York: Oxford University Press, 2002.
Paul A. Schewe, ed.	*Preventing Violence in Relationships: Interventions Across the Life Span.* Washington, DC: American Psychological Association, 2002.
Elizabeth M. Schneider	*Battered Women and Feminist Lawmaking.* New Haven, CT: Yale University Press, 2000.
Donald Stewart	*Refuge: A Pathway Out of Domestic Violence and Abuse.* Birmingham, AL: New Hope, 2004.
Julie Taylor-Browne, ed.	*What Works in Reducing Domestic Violence?* London, UK: Whiting & Birch, 2002.
Elaine Weiss	*Family and Friends' Guide to Domestic Violence.* Volcano, CA: Volcano, 2003.
Susan Weitzman	*"Not to People Like Us": Hidden Abuse in Upscale Marriages.* New York: Basic Books, 2001.
Evelyn C. White	*Chain, Chain, Change: For Black Women in Abusive Relationships.* 2nd ed. Emeryville, CA: Seal Press/Avalon, 1995.

Periodicals

Stephanie Angelo	"Firms Should Be on Alert for Domestic Abuse," *Tucson Citizen*, October 15, 2004.
Larry W. Bennett	"Substance Abuse and Women Abuse by Male Partners," National Resource Center on Domestic Violence, February 1998. http://www.vawnet.org/DomesticViolence/Research/VawnetDocs/ARsubstance.pdf.

Madeleine Brindley	"Men Left in Shadows by Plague of Domestic Violence," *Cardiff (Wales) Western Mail*, October 30, 2002.
Cindy Carcano	"Immigrant Women in Abusive Relationships Rarely Seek Out Help," *Orange County Register*, February 15, 2005.
Kathleen Carlin	"Measuring Success: Evaluating Batterers Intervention Programs," Men Stopping Violence, 2001. www.menstoppingviolence.org/LearnMore/articles/MeasuringSuccess.pdf.
Barbara Dehl	"'This Guy Is Going to Kill My Daughter,'" *Good Housekeeping*, April 2003.
Maria Duffy, Aimee Nolan, and Dave Scruggs	"Addressing Issues of Domestic Violence Through Community Supervision of Offenders," *Corrections Today*, February 2003.
Patricia Eng	"Safety and Justice for All," Ms. Foundation for Women, 2003. www.ms.foundation.org/user-assets/PDF/Program/safetyjustice.pdf.
William Fisher	"Rights—U.S.: Battered Women Seeking Asylum Face Legal Quagmire," Inter Press Service, February 15, 2005.
Loretta Frederick and Kristine C. Lizdas	"The Role of Restorative Justice in the Women's Movement," Battered Women's Justice Project, September 2003. www.bwjp.org/documents/finalrj.pdf.
Rus Ervin Funk	"Preventing Sexist Violence: Are We Doing What We Need to Be Doing?" Michigan Coalition Against Sexual and Domestic Violence, November 8, 2002. www.ncdsv.org/images/PreventingSADV2.pdf.
Kate Gurnett	"Orders Don't Always Protect," *Albany (N.Y.) Times Union*, February 27, 2005.
Johann Hari	"Now Men Are the Silent Victims of Domestic Violence," *London Independent*, October 24, 2003.
Harvard Mental Health Letter	"Countering Domestic Violence," April 2004.
Laila Karamally	"Companies Try to Bring Domestic Violence Issues into the Open," *Workforce Management*, September 1, 2004.
David M. Kennedy	"Rethinking Law Enforcement Strategies to Prevent Domestic Violence," *Networks* (National Center for Victims of Crime), Spring/Summer 2004.
Legal Momentum	"The Impact of Violence in the Lives of Working Women," Legal Momentum, 2002. www.legalmomentum.org/pub/pubs/CreatingSolutions.pdf.

Susan Lewis — "Ten Years of VAWA: Strengthening Anti-Sexual Violence Work," *Resource* (National Sexual Violence Resource Center), Spring/Summer 2004.

Elizabeth C. McCord — "Medical Screening in Rural Areas," *Resource* (National Sexual Violence Resource Center), Spring/Summer 2004.

Fernando Mederos, Denise Gamache, and Ellen Pence — "Domestic Violence and Probation," Battered Women's Justice Project. www.bwjp.org/documents/probationV.htm.

Joan Meier — "Battered Justice for Battered Women," *Washington Post*, March 19, 2005.

Occupational Health Management — "Program Targets Domestic Violence: Employee Attitudes Shift," July 2004.

Linda A. Osmundson — "Sisters, We're Doin' It to Ourselves," *Off Our Backs*, December 2001.

Joanna Pearl — "Battered," *Community Care*, July 22, 2004.

William S. Pollack — "Preventing Violence Through Family Connection," *Brown University Child and Adolescent Behavior Letter*, December 2001.

Nancy Poole and Lorraine Greaves — "Women's Shelters, Substance Use and Domestic Violence," *Journal of Addiction and Mental Health*, Summer 2004.

Abigail Pugh — "Beyond Shame and Blame: New Approach Needed for Treating Domestically Violent Men," *Journal of Addiction and Mental Health*, Winter 2003.

Mallika Punukollu — "Domestic Violence: Screening Made Practical," *Journal of Family Practice*, July 2003.

Bill Reiter — "Silent, Scared Prisoners," *Des Moines Register*, February 27, 2005.

Ann Rosewater — "Promoting Prevention, Targeting Teens: An Emerging Agenda to Reduce Domestic Violence," Family Violence Prevention Fund, July 2003. http://endabuse.org/field/PromotingPrevention1003.pdf.

SaraKay Smullins — "Counseling the Clergy on How to Help Victims of Domestic Violence," *Annals of the American Psychotherapy Association*, November/December 2001.

Kiersten Stewart — "Uncle Sam Wants You to Get Married," *Gadflyer*, September 14, 2004.

Ann Taket et al. — "Routinely Asking Women About Domestic Violence in Health Settings," *British Medical Journal*, September 20, 2003.

Beverly Younger Urban	"Evaluation Report: Harman International Domestic Violence Prevention Project," Family Violence Prevention Fund, 2004. http://endabuse.org/field/HarmanReport.pdf.
U.S. Preventive Services Task Force	"Screening for Family and Intimate Partner Violence: Recommendation Statement," *American Family Physician*, August 15, 2004.
Nikki van der Gaag	"The Other Side of Silence," *New Internationalist*, November 2004.

Index